'Allan Harman's v   introduction to the Ol   noteworthy for its red   that focuses on the co   Old Testament. Many people have been greatly influenced by theologies that teach the discontinuity of the Scriptures – Harman's book correctly counters those false approaches. This is a work that I will give to new Christians and to those who have little understanding of a Reformed perspective to the Hebrew Bible. It is a very helpful work.'

John Currid
Reformed Theological Seminary
Jackson, Mississippi
USA

ISBN 1 85792 509 2

Cover design by Owen Daily

LEARNING
ABOUT
THE OLD
TESTAMENT

Allan M. Harman

Christian Focus

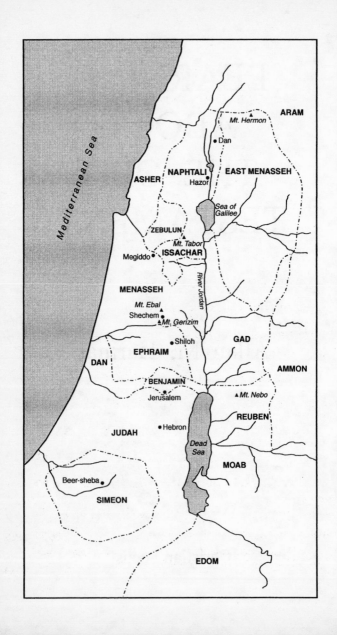

Contents

1

APPROACHING THE
OLD TESTAMENT

Our Attitude to the Old Testament
When we take up a copy of the Old Testament, it is important to recognise that we must approach our reading and study of it in a different way from other ancient books. It claims to be God's Word and demands our obedience. It is to be treasured and obeyed because of its origin and character. Only by God's Holy Spirit are we convinced of this because God's Word comes to us as sinners.

Our attitude to it can be summed up in this way. We have to come to it

with reverence – it is God's Word as spoken and written by his servants, and it is to be handled and used with reverence.

with devotion – it is a book which speaks of the wonderful truths about God and his works. Also it contains many passages of praise which we can echo in our worship.

with obedience – it is a revelation of God's character and of his demands upon his children. The basic laws of the Old Testament carry over into the New Testament.

The Text of the Bible

Our main goal should be to get to know the text of the Old Testament. We cannot interpret the Old Testament without reading it! There is no substitute for this deep acquaintance with the 39 books which make up the Old Testament.

Over the centuries God preserved the Scriptures in their original languages and brought the manuscripts down to the present day. With meticulous care the Jewish scribes transmitted the Hebrew text to their successors. There is little variation between extant manuscripts of the Old Testament, a fact reinforced by the finding of the Dead Sea Scrolls. These finds, dating from 1945 onwards, took the history of the Old Testament text back 1000 years to before the time of Christ.

Bible Translations

The need for translations of the Hebrew Old Testament became apparent before Christian times. The first Greek translation was made in Alexandria in Egypt, reputedly by 72 men brought down from Palestine. This legendary origin of this translation is reflected in the name by which it is still known, the Septuagint (Greek for 70). It virtually became the Bible of the early Christian church, for Greek was the *lingua franca* (common language) of the Mediterranean world. Other translations into languages such as Aramaic, Syriac, Arabic and especially Latin followed. The Latin Bible, translated by Jerome and called the Vulgate, meaning the common version, was used by the church in medieval times and is still the official Bible of the Roman Catholic Church to the present day.

Once missionary work began, there was a need for translations into many languages. At the time of the Reformation the major European languages became the vehicles for transmitting God's Word. In English, the Authorised or King James Version was a major achievement and remained as a standard English version for over 350 years. Various revisions of it are now available including the Revised Standard Version, The New American Standard Bible, and the New King James Version. The New International Version is a completely new translation into modern English. The Good News Bible is in more colloquial English, but lacks the accuracy necessary for study purposes. For our own use we need to pick one of the new versions and make it our Bible for regular reading and study. Constant changing between versions militates against acquiring a thorough knowledge of the English text of the Bible.

Perspective on the Study of the Old Testament
Certain general principles need to be in our minds as we come to the study of the Old Testament. Without these principles we will become engrossed with difficult detail, make wrong application of laws, or fail to grasp the major themes.

It is essential to remember the unity of the Bible.

Though composed of sixty-six books, the Bible forms a unity. It contains God's revelation given over a long period of time. However, the ultimate author of the Bible is God himself, and the theme which is central to it concerns himself and his relationship with the world he made. When any particular passage proves difficult to understand, we must turn to other passages where the truth is set out more plainly.

Guidelines

In studying the Old Testament revelation there are three main ideas about it which help to provide guidelines for us.

1. God's revelation was progressive, for he did not reveal himself fully until the coming of Jesus. This is not to say that early revelation was false, and the later revelation true. Rather, the progression was from partial to complete, from preparatory to final.

2. God's revelation came in stages, and the Old Testament itself provides the markers which set off several major periods of revelation from each other. When we look at the history of the Old Testament we can see periods (such as the Exodus from Egypt) when God did so much for Israel and also revealed so much of his character and purpose.

3. God's revelation was redemptive, for the main purpose of revelation was to show how sinners can be redeemed and brought back into fellowship with God. Believers in the Old Testament enjoyed

that experience of redemption as much as New Testament Christians.

The light of the New Testament is necessary to understand the Old Testament. It is the final revelation of God, and teaches us many aspects of earlier revelation. In it we find explanations given of practices and institutions, and above all we are taught how Jesus has fulfilled what was given in sign language. God, who spoke in many different ways by his prophets, spoke finally in the coming of Jesus (Heb. 1:1-2). Without the New Testament, our reading of the Old Testament would be like trying to understand a novel or play without having the final chapter to help us. The expectation of the Old Testament believers finds its fulfilment in the person and ministry of Jesus.

Importance of the Old Testament
Study of the Old Testament is important for Christians today. The foundational truths of the Bible are set out in the Old Testament, and in many cases are pre-supposed by the New Testament writers. Without a knowledge of the Old Testament, we cannot adequately explain much of the New Testament. While this applies particularly to books like the Epistle to the Hebrews, yet it also applies very widely to words and concepts which are rooted in the Old Testament.

Two other comments need to be made. The first is that to understand the Old Testament we cannot be selective in our reading of its pages. The total flow of the history and thought of that period must be in our minds if we are to understand it for ourselves. Knowledge of isolated stories does not give us the broad perspective which we need.

Secondly, as our understanding of the Old Testament increases, it should also increase our understanding of the New Testament. Moreover, our increasing biblical knowledge should stimulate us to go and tell the message of the Bible to others. Biblical study should result in the desire to bring others to share both our knowledge and our commitment to the Lord.

2

BACKGROUND TO
THE OLD TESTAMENT

The Setting of the Old Testament

The Old Testament was written in the Near East,
and so it has many features which reflect the various
cultural backgrounds from which it came. Study of
these backgrounds helps us to understand customs
which are referred to in the biblical text, and also
words and phrases which mention things which are
strange to us. The fact that God's revelation came
in particular cultural settings need not surprise us,
for the events of the Bible happened on actual
calendar days and in precise geographical situations.
The more we know about these situations, the better
we are able to understand the significance of words
and events. The development of modern
archaeology has been of great assistance in shedding
light on the ancient Near East.

Palestine was situated on the Mediterranean
coast in a strategic part of the Near East. The name
'Palestine' has been taken over into English from
the word 'Philistia', land of the Philistines. It was
on convenient trade routes between Egypt in the
south west and countries such as Assyria in the north
east. While we may think the climate harsh and the
vegetation anything but lush, the Bible describes it
as a land flowing with milk and honey. In

comparison with neighbouring countries it was well-provided with water supplies and other natural advantages. From the Mediterranean coast and also from the Gulf of Aqaba there was sea access to other sources of supply of precious goods.

The Geography of Palestine

The biblical text calls the name of the land Canaan, after its inhabitants prior to the Israelite invasion. The land was promised to Abraham by God, and descriptions of its boundaries are given in various Old Testament passages (Gen. 15:18-21; Josh. 1:4; Ps. 80:8-11). Basically these boundaries were Egypt in the south, Lebanon in the north, the Mediterranean in the west and the Euphrates in the east. This territory was occupied in at least two periods of Old Testament history. During the reigns of David and Solomon the kingdom was extended to the promised borders; and then later, during the reigns of Jeroboam II in the north and Uzziah in the south, the full territorial lands were under Israelite control.

The land of Canaan has four main geographical areas, all running north/south. The first is the rich coastal plain, broken only by the Carmel range jutting out to the sea. Secondly, there is the upland area stretching from the hills of Galilee in the north, down through Samaria, and finally embracing the Judean hills in the south. The only major break in this line of hills is where the valley of Jezreel extends from the Mediterranean just north of the

Carmel range to the Jordan in the east. Thirdly, there is the Jordan valley, from Hermon in the north down to the Sea of Galilee, and from there the Jordan meanders down to the Dead Sea. The Jordan today in this stretch has very little water in it, because its resources are tapped further north to provide water for much of Israel's irrigation system. The surface level of the Dead Sea is well below sea level (400 metres), with the floor at the deepest part being another 400 metres lower still. The sea has a very high salt content, which prevents any life existing in it, and from which it got its biblical name, 'The Salt Sea'. South of the Dead Sea the same rift valley continues down to the present day port and tourist resort of Eilat. The fourth region is that of the hills of Transjordania, including Golan, Bashan, and Moab.

The geography of Palestine is important because it helps to explain many references and incidents in the Old Testament. For example, the study of a map of Palestine shows why sites such as those occupied by Jerusalem or Samaria were chosen. These sites were strategic ones with good natural defences. The geography dictated the trade routes, and this helps to explain why a king such as Josiah should be killed by the Egyptians at Megiddo in the valley of Jezreel (2 Kings 23:29,30).

The Archaeology of Palestine
The limitations of archaeological discovery have to be recognised at the outset. In the Old Testament there is no continuous historical record which notes

every major event. There are many gaps in our knowledge, and we must also remember that we are dealing with a Near Eastern text, not a Western one. This means that we cannot impose our criteria of historical writing on the Old Testament. Thus it is a difficult task on many occasions to align the Old Testament record with the present state of knowledge derived from archaeology.

Another real limitation is that archaeology will never be able to provide convincing proof for the accuracy of the Old Testament. Two main reasons lie behind this statement. On the one hand, not every important site, or any site in its entirety, will ever be excavated. The task is just too extensive to allow that to happen. A tremendous amount of work has been done, but an even greater amount of evidence awaits investigation. On the other hand, archaeology can never provide proof of much of the Old Testament because it is composed of material not subject to proof. That is to say, much of the Old Testament is comprised of words which are claimed to be from God or spoken by his servants the prophets. These words are not susceptible to proof by archaeological discovery.

The purpose of archaeology for the Old Testament is not primarily to confirm the accuracy of the text. Some of the reasons for this have already been given. There is a more basic reason in that God's Word cannot be proved by means of this kind. To say that we have to prove the Bible's accuracy before we believe it, is to place something in a position as judge of the Bible. The Bible claims to be God's Word and we have to accept it on the basis of its own testimony and as the Holy Spirit confirms this to our hearts. No human judge can determine its claims.

The Main Aim of Archaeology
The main task of archaeology is to illuminate the Old Testament. This means that we look to archaeology to explain things which were difficult for us to understand before we had access to archaeological discoveries. It helps by clarifying the meaning of something which was previously obscure. Several good examples occur in the patriarchal narratives, such as the custom of a childless couple adopting a servant as an heir (Gen. 15:2-3), which, according to documents from Ur and Nuzi, was a common practice.

Archaeology also helps by illustrating what we already know. It makes more vivid things we already understand, by providing examples which we can see or feel. What is observed in this way impresses the matters more firmly in our minds and gives us further parallels or background information. To visit a museum with a display of objects from the biblical world enables us to visualise to a greater degree what the every-day life of the people was like. To be able to visit Israel and see major excavations brings a new dimension to our understanding of many parts of the Old Testament.

While the role of archaeology is not primarily to prove the Bible, archaeology does help by demonstrating the reliability and accuracy of the biblical writings. The biblical faith rests on the historical basis of the Bible. Advancing knowledge of archaeology provides complementary information from outside the Bible, and nothing has been found which can be proved to contradict any assertion in the biblical text. Archaeology itself is a developing discipline, and former investigations require verification and re-assessment. Archaeological research will continue to provide valuable help as we seek to understand what God has given us in the pages of the Old Testament.

3

GOD'S COVENANTS

Covenants in the Old Testament

We are very used to the word 'covenant', because
we often hear it in connection with the Lord's
Supper: 'This is the blood of the new covenant
which is shed for many.' Another synonym is the
word 'testament', which is common in the New
Testament, occurring over thirty times in our
English Bibles. Not only does the word 'covenant'
occur frequently, but the concept is of great
significance for understanding the Bible. It provides
the markers which distinguish the various periods
of biblical history and revelation.

In the Old Testament, 'covenant' is used of
formal relationships between people, such as the
one between David and Jonathan (1 Sam. 18:3).
However, the term is used most frequently to
describe the relationship between God and men. In
quite a few cases there is a ceremony in which God
and the people entering into the covenant
relationship give assent to the demands of the
covenant, or pledge performance of certain duties.
Thus we have a passage such as Genesis 15, which
describes a vision of God ratifying the covenant he
had made with Abraham. Exodus 24 provides an
illustration of a covenant where the people pledge
their obedience to the Lord's demands. Right
through the Old Testament, from the first book

(Genesis) to the last one in our Bibles (Malachi), there is constant mention of God's covenant with his people.

Covenants outside the Bible

Like many other biblical words and ideas, that of covenant is one which was well-known to people in the ancient Near East. Archaeology has helped here, in providing tablets from various countries which detail how kings made covenants or treaties with conquered peoples. These treaties date from as early as 2300 BC down to 700 BC. In particular, treaties made by the Hittites in the period just before the Israelites came out of their bondage in Egypt show many similarities to those in the Old Testament. These treaties follow a set form which takes on this appearance:

a. An introduction explaining who the king is.
b. An historical survey explaining the background to the treaty.
c. Demands which the king made upon his subjects.
d. Provision for a copy to be placed in the temple of the people and for the regular reading of it.
e. Calling witnesses to bear testimony to the fact that the treaty had been made.
f. Curses or blessings which would follow, depending upon obedience or disobedience.

In addition to these features, which were provided in writing, there was also an oath. This was usually taken by following some set ritual.

Several Old Testament covenants show very strong resemblances to this pattern. This is so when we look at the covenant made with Abraham (Gen. 12, 15, 17), or the covenant at Sinai (Exod. 20-24), or the renewal of that covenant forty years later just before the children of Israel marched into the land of Canaan (the book of Deuteronomy). What happened was that God chose to give his teaching to Israel in a form with which they were already quite familiar. By using ideas from the secular realm and applying them in the spiritual realm, God was helping the people to grasp more easily the significance of their relationship with himself. He was the great king who had redeemed Israel from slavery in Egypt to become his devoted servants.

Covenant in the New Testament
The first appearances of the idea of the 'covenant' in the New Testament are in Luke 1, in the songs of Mary (the Magnificat) and of Zechariah (the Benedictus). Both sing of how Jesus' coming fulfils the covenant made so long before with Abraham. The word appears in the accounts of the Last Supper, in the epistle to the Galatians, and most frequently in the epistle to the Hebrews. The nature of a covenant clearly remains the same in both Old and New Testaments. The stress is on the wonderful grace of a sovereign God who comes to meet sinners in their need and enters into this relationship with them.

The English Bibles use the word 'testament' (i.e. a will) to translate the word for 'covenant' which appears in the Greek New Testament. This is probably because of the way it is used in Hebrews 9:16,17, where the idea of a will is definitely present. However, this is the only passage in the New Testament where we have to avoid the English word 'covenant'. Even here the same idea as a covenant is seen, in that there is no mention of an arrangement entered into after mutual discussion. Rather, the idea is that Jesus chose how his death would bring blessings to his faithful followers. As with the Old Testament, the New Testament speaks of how God stooped to help those who were helpless, and how he brought into being a new covenant through the blood of Jesus.

Definition of Covenant

It helps us to understand the idea better if we attempt to give a definition of it. We have to look at the way the Bible uses the idea, and then state this clearly in a few words. It is an idea connected with a relationship that God establishes. He normally gave promises in connection with a covenant, and the people had to pledge themselves to obey his commands. Thus we can say that a covenant is a bond between God and man, given by a sovereign God as an expression of his grace, and in this formal way he expresses the relationship which exists between them. To be in a covenant relationship with God is a great blessing, for God promises, 'I will be your God and you shall be my people.'

Sometimes the Bible speaks about a covenant

without using the precise word. This is because other words also suggested the idea, and terms like 'chose' or 'know' often come in contexts which are describing some aspect of God's covenant. In Amos 3:2, God charges his own people with their sin and says, 'You only have I known of all the families of the earth.' This is clearly a reference back to God's choice of Israel and to the covenant which he made at Sinai. In 2 Samuel 7 God makes wonderful promises to King David, but nowhere in this passage is the word 'covenant' used. However, it is clear that it is a covenant, for when all the ideas are put into song in Psalm 89, the word 'covenant' appears several times (see verses 3, 28, 34, 39). Likewise the early chapters of Genesis have to be understood as a covenant. This is shown by the fact that the covenant with Noah only confirms the earlier covenant (Gen. 6:18), and the New Testament supports that by the way in which it links Adam and Jesus together as covenant mediators (Rom. 5:12ff.; 1 Cor. 15:21-22, 45-49).

The people in the Old Testament were very familiar with the covenant idea. In the psalms and in the writings of the prophets the idea comes to the fore in many ways. From beginning to end the Old Testament reveals an understanding of God's steadfast covenant mercies. All the literature of the Old Testament speaks of the covenant, and the idea is used to point forward to the coming of a new covenant when Jesus comes as Messiah (Jer. 31:31-34; cf. Heb. 8:8-12).

4

THE COVENANT OF CREATION

The Declaration of God's Lordship

The Bible opens in a very dramatic way. It presents us with a creator who made this world out of nothing. He only has to speak and things come into existence (cf. Pss. 33:6; 148:5). Throughout the first chapter of Genesis, God's activity follows a pattern. He declares what he is going to do, then gives his command, the creative activity takes place, and finally he pronounces it 'good'. In the context 'good' is not contrasted with 'bad'. Rather, it indicates that God looked over his creation and saw that what had come into being corresponded with his purpose. The whole narrative in Genesis stresses the sovereign creator who brings everything into being by his great power.

Everything that was created was for a purpose. Thus God designates the role of the sun and moon (Gen. 1:16-18) and the dominion which man is to have over the rest of the created world (Gen. 1:28). All creation is directed to fulfilling his will, and every aspect of it should point to its origin and Lord. The song of the 24 elders in Revelation is a beautiful expression of this idea: 'You are worthy, our Lord and God, to receive glory and honour and power, for you created all things, and by your will they were created and have their being' (Rev. 4:11).

The Creation of Man

The account of creation presents us with a series of days. Nowhere does the Bible fix the length of these days, and in Genesis 1 and 2 the word 'day' is used in at least four different senses. There is a general parallel between the first three days and the second three days. On the first three were created light, sea and air, and finally land and vegetation. Then on the second three days we have the created things which rule over these realms – light bearers (sun, moon and stars), fish and fowl, and finally animals and man. The creation of man forms the climax of God's creative work. In Psalm 8, a song dealing with creation, it is not surprising that the psalmist, after looking at the world around him, exclaims, 'What is man that you are mindful of him, the son of man that you care for him? You made him a little lower than the heavenly beings and crowned him with glory and honour' (Ps. 8:4-5).

While man is a creature of God like the animals, yet the difference between them is marked. Man was made in God's image and likeness (Gen. 1:26). Man has a soul and mind, and he was created to have fellowship with God. The New Testament helps to explain what is meant by the image of God when it speaks of us being restored in Christ to God's image in righteousness and holiness (Eph. 4:24; Col. 3:10).

Man was appointed to rule in God's stead over the created world. His task was to populate the earth and to have dominion over it (Gen. 1:28). As the apex of creation, man was invested with authority. Psalm 8:6 expresses it in praise to God in this way: 'You made him ruler over the works of your hands; you put everything under his feet.' This general command in Genesis 1 is made more explicit when Adam is placed in the Garden of Eden 'to work it and take care of it' (Gen. 2:15). He has delegated authority from God over creation, but this means caring for the creation as God himself would. The earth is man's to use wisely.

Man's original position in relation to God was one of fellowship and communion. This is shown by the fact that man was living in Eden, God's garden. In that garden there was the tree of life (Gen. 2:9), which will appear again in heaven when sin is no more (Rev. 2:7). Also, the garden was the place where God revealed himself to man by speaking with him and appearing to him. There was nothing to mar the relationship between himself and his creator.

Temptation and Sin
In the sinless life of Eden a tempter appeared. The Bible does not explain the origin of evil. Rather, just as it confronts us with the Creator in Genesis 1, so it confronts us with Satan in Genesis 3. While God had a good design in view in allowing Adam and Eve to be tempted, Satan had an evil design. He wanted them to acknowledge him as lord of their lives, and in order to achieve that, he allured them away from commitment to God. The Bible often

refs to the reality of this experience and to the reality of the Devil (cf. the New Testament references in Matt. 13:38,39; John 8:44; Rom. 16:20; 2 Cor. 11:14; 1 John 3:8; Rev. 12:9).

Satan worked cleverly in tempting Adam and Eve. He approached Eve first, and put in her mind the thought that God's prohibition of eating of the fruit was too comprehensive. When Eve began to doubt God's word, Satan flatly contradicted his statements, and he tempted Eve to think she could be like God himself (Gen. 3:4-5). When Eve was attracted to the fruit of the tree as desirable to her sight, appealing to taste, and as able to make her wise, she yielded to the tempter. Sin still has its attraction for sinners (Jas. 1:13-14; 1 John 2:15-16). In turn Eve became the agent in tempting Adam, and he too succumbed.

Sin brought with it immediate consequences. Being sinners, Adam and Eve were then no longer in fellowship with God. They realised they needed covering when in God's presence, and they tried to make garments for themselves, and even to hide themselves when he appeared. What was needed was the covering which God would provide for them (Gen. 3:21). They now lost their happy relationship with God, and surrendered their right to be in God's garden (see Gen. 3:23-24). The fact that they were sinners showed itself, with Adam even blaming Eve, whom he got from God, for his sin (Gen. 3:12).

Curse and Blessing

Sin always brings judgement. So it was with the first sin. Immediately after interrogating Adam and Eve, God pronounced judgement. That judgement affected Satan, woman, and man. God's curse was expressed against Satan, who would be subjected to degradation. Those who followed him would have life-long antagonism towards those who trusted in God's word. Human life was to continue, but relationships would be distorted, and child-bearing and production of necessary foodstuffs would now become arduous. The effect of sin was not to introduce a new principle (death), but to alter the existing relationships so that life became burdensome. Death, instead of working for man's good, was now to apply to man himself. As soon as sin came, man was spiritually dead and subject also to physical death. Both Old and New Testaments teach that God is able to give new spiritual life, and that in Christ he has taken the sting out of death for Christian believers (1 Cor. 15:54-57).

But as well as judgement there was hope. Though Adam and Eve were banished from the garden, God's grace was extended to them, and this grace was expressed in various ways. When the account describes how God provided garments and clothed them, it is emphasising that it was God who moved to meet man in his need. When Eve bore Cain she acknowledged that that was with the help of the Lord (Gen. 4:1). However, the greatest promise was that the offspring of the woman would crush the head of the serpent (Gen. 3:15). Martin Luther called this the first proclamation of the gospel. It held out the prospect that ultimately the seed of the woman, in the person of the Messiah, would crush Satan. That happened on the Cross, when Jesus disarmed the Satanic powers and authorities and made a public spectacle of them (Col. 2:15). The final vanquishing of Satan is yet to come (Rom. 16:20; Rev. 20:7-10).

5

THE COVENANT WITH NOAH

The Progress of Sin

The account in Genesis gives some positive
indications of the faith and hope of mankind after
the coming of sin. The first child born bears the
name Cain, because, his mother said, he had been
born with the help of the Lord (Gen. 4:1). Seth, the
name given to the third son (Gen. 4:25), contrasts
the sin of Cain in killing Abel with what God put in
his place (Seth means 'put'). Worship of God is
expressly mentioned in the reference to men calling
on the name of the Lord (Gen. 4:26). But the
consciousness of the effects of sin seems to have
been present, for when Noah is born, Lamech, his
father, said: 'Out of the ground which the LORD has
cursed this one shall bring us relief from our work
and from the toil of our hands' (Gen. 5:29). The
earlier part of chapter 5 has been concerned with
the genealogy of Adam. Just as God had created
him in his image (Gen. 1:26), so Adam procreates
in his own image (Gen. 5:3). However, the
genealogy states one of the effects of sin, in that it
tells that each person mentioned died. The only
exception to this was the godly Enoch, whom God
took away without his passing through death.

The general picture given of human life is one
of degeneration and rebellion against God. Thus,

Cain kills his brother, and is condemned to wander about like a vagrant (Gen. 4:1-16). By the time the seventh generation is reached with Lamech, God's provisions for man, as set out in chapter 1, are abused. Lamech takes two wives, and proudly boasts of killing a young man who wounded him (Gen. 4:19, 23-24). His character is in marked contrast to his opposite number in the line of Seth, Enoch, who walked with God (Gen. 5:22,24).

The degeneration reached its climax in the situation described in Genesis 6:1-7. The best interpretation of the early verses in this section is that rulers (called 'sons of God') were engaging in polygamy (marrying whom they would). Because they long for a name (i.e. a reputation, v. 4), they abuse their office and allow their sinful desires to go contrary to God's ordinances. Like their forefather Lamech, they will not be constrained by God's basic pattern for human life.

Noah, the Covenant Servant

The character of Noah is important, for he was a righteous man, being set apart from his own generation by his blameless life (Gen. 6:9). He had a very close relationship with God which is described, as in Enoch's case, by the words 'walking with God'. As far as God's commands were concerned he was obedient, and carried out explicitly the instructions he was given (see Gen. 6:22; 7:5, 16).

God in his grace came to Noah and warned him

of his impending judgement upon the world because of man's sin. Wickedness had multiplied, and men were perpetually turning to evil (Gen. 6:5, 11). Noah was instructed to make an ark to save his family and the animals which God specified. The New Testament points out that Noah acted out of faith, because he could not see the things of which he was warned. However, his obedient action was in itself an act condemning the world for its sin and unbelief (Heb. 11:7).

The relationship between himself and Noah was called a covenant by God, who said that he was confirming *his* covenant. Hence we have commands given in Genesis 1 re-issued to Noah at the time of the flood (Gen. 9:1,7). Despite the sinful condition of mankind, God intended to maintain the covenant relationship. The stress on God's initiative in the matter becomes even clearer from Genesis 9, where God emphasises in verses 9-17 that the origin of the relationship was with himself.

The account of the flood is given in Genesis 7:1-8:19. The description of the flood permits one to interpret it either as a flood universal in extent, or else a flood which was geographically more limited but which destroyed all living creatures. At present the evidence seems to favour the latter, with geological investigation supporting massive local floods but not a universal one. The Bible stresses that the flood was God's instrument of judgement and that every living creature, except those in the ark, perished (Gen. 7:21-23; 2 Pet. 3:6-7).

The New Order

God in his grace preserved all who were in the ark. He 'remembered' them (Gen. 8:1) and brought them out of the ark. God's concern was for mankind, but also for all the animals in the ark. They too were the objects of his mercy and included within the covenant he was making (Gen. 8:21; 9:9-10, cf. Ps. 104:27-28; 145:9, 15-16; Jon. 4:11). His grace was to continue till the end of time (note the double occurrence of 'never again' in Gen. 8:21), while the Lord indicates that the earth is not going to endure for ever (v. 22).

The reason why God would not again destroy the world in this way is given in verse 21: 'Never again will I curse the ground because of man, even though every inclination of his heart is evil from childhood.' This may seem surprising because it is practically the same as the reason given in Genesis 6:5 for the coming of the judgment of the flood. Man's sinful heart was not changed by the flood, but remained the same. It was going to take something quite different to alter it. Later in the Bible we learn of the way in which God would give a new heart (Ezek. 36:26) and recreate to make all things new (2 Cor. 5:17).

After the flood God gave very clear directions regarding several aspects of human life.

Human life was to continue, and would never again be destroyed in the way it had been. In particular, the command given to man in

Genesis 1:28 to populate the earth is now repeated twice (Gen. 9:1,7). Sin would continue to manifest itself in the form of violence against other human beings.

Human life was precious, because man was made in God's image. All life is God's, but especially human life. Therefore, to attack a fellow man was the same as attacking God. Provision was made for society to control acts against other humans, with the basic principle being that the punishment must not exceed the crime (Gen. 9:5-6).

Human life was to be sustained. This is implied in the command to fill the earth, but specific provision is made for man's physical needs (Gen. 9:2-3). Sin brought disturbance into the natural world, but still the basic situation of Genesis 1 was to continue, in that man was to have dominion and be able to use everything in God's world.

In confirming his covenant, God also gave a sign. The rainbow, chosen now as the sign of God's covenant (Gen. 9:12-17), was probably already in existence, but it was given new meaning as it was consecrated to serve in this particular way. Its main reference is not to us but to God, for he sees it and remembers his covenant. God cannot forget, but this sign emphasised how absolute God's promises were. Because it is a sign visible to us, it also reminds us of God's promises not to destroy the world again as happened in the flood. The Hebrew word used in this passage for 'rainbow' is the usual word for a battle-bow, and so there may be present the idea that after the storm of the flood God is setting aside his judgement and showing his mercy and grace. When the Lord spoke through Isaiah of his promise that the waters would not again cover the earth, he promised that 'my unfailing love for you will not be shaken nor my covenant of peace be removed' (Isa. 54:9-10).

6

THE COVENANT WITH ABRAHAM

The Call of Abraham

The God of glory appeared to Abram (meaning 'exalted father', but renamed Abraham, 'father of many', Gen. 17:5) in his home in Ur. He was instructed to go out and proceed to the land which God would show him (Gen. 12:1). That meant first of all going to Haran, situated north-west from Ur. There he stayed until the death of his father Terah, when he set out with his wife and his nephew Lot for the land of Canaan to the south-west of Haran. The earliest translation of the Old Testament (the Greek Septuagint of about 250 BC) rightly calls him 'Abraham the migrant'. Although he did not know where he was going when first called, Abraham obeyed, and 'by faith he made his home in the promised land like a stranger in a foreign country' (Heb. 11:9). As with the earlier covenants, it is God who takes the initiative and makes known his commands and promises to Abraham.

Behind the call of Abraham lay the desire of God to have a people who would be separated from others as his own special people. God called him to leave the culture and community he knew so well. He was to become a recipient of God's revelation, and in order to be a channel of knowledge of the true God he had to forsake the culture in which he had been raised. From the outset Abraham had to learn that there is a distinctiveness about commitment to the living God. Severing himself from home and family, he had to make Jehovah alone his support and stay.

God's Covenant with Abraham

The covenant God made with Abraham is probably the one covenant referred to more often than any others in the Bible. There are three chapters in Genesis (12, 15, 17) which deal with this covenant. Perhaps chapter 12 anticipates the very important covenant ceremony detailed in chapter 15, while chapter 17 amounts to a confirmation of what has already been promised. Chapter 15 has a ceremony, in which God, in visible form, passes between dismembered pieces of animals. This type of ceremony was well-known as a way of taking an oath in the ancient Near East. In this case God was pledging himself to fulfil all that he had promised to do for Abraham.

Abraham was given something far more than just an inward sense of God's call. His religious life rested on great objective facts, for God promised certain things to his faithful servant. The stress was not on what Abraham would do for God, but what God would do for Abraham. All these promises involved great faith on Abraham's part, and he was tested in regard to each one. They were:

that the chosen family was going to become a great nation (Gen. 12:2; 15:4-5; 17:5-6). He and Sarai (later called Sarah, Gen. 17:15) at that time were childless, but they were strengthened in faith and were persuaded that God had the power to do what he had promised (Rom. 4:20-21; Heb. 11:11-12). Abraham declared his Amen to what God promised, and it was counted to him for righteousness (Gen. 15:6; cf. Rom. 4:3, 9). This was the first of the promises fulfilled. God gave them Isaac, and then many descendants.

that the land of Canaan was to be his family's possession (Gen. 12:7; 15:7; 17:8). This territory extended from the river of Egypt to Lebanon, from the Mediterranean to the Euphrates (cf. Josh. 1:4), and it was occupied during the reigns of David and Solomon, and later in the divided Kingdom when Jeroboam II ruled over Israel and Uzziah ruled over Judah. From Genesis 12 onwards the theme of the land is a major concern, until the conquest is recorded in the book of Joshua.

that in Abraham all the families of the earth would be blessed (Gen. 12:2-3; 22:18; 26:4). Some of the references to this blessing suggest that people would ask God to bless them just as he had blessed Abraham. Most references to it, however, imply that through Abraham's descendants God would bring blessing to the nations. The New Testament tells us this is what happened when Jesus came (Gal. 3:14).

These covenant promises to Abraham were repeated to Isaac (Gen. 26:2-5, 24) and Jacob (Gen. 28:13-15; 35:9-12). The three names are often linked together when reference is made to these great promises (e.g. in Exod. 2:24; 3:6, 15f.; Deut. 9:27; 2 Kings 13:23; Ps. 105:6-11).

The Rite of Circumcision
As a sign of this covenant God commanded the rite of circumcision to be performed on all the males in Abraham's family, and thereafter on all male children. If obedience was not shown to this requirement, then death would follow. The language used plays on the fact that the expression in Hebrew for 'make a covenant' is really 'cut a covenant'. Thus the penalty was being cut off from Israel, so that it was no longer just a token sign, but the real thing. Thus the sign was a token one carried in the flesh of every male Israelite. It was a constant reminder of the need to keep God's covenant, and thus enjoy his blessing, or else suffer the consequences of disobedience. Later in the Bible the idea of circumcision was used in a wider sense. The heart had to be circumcised before God, for ultimately a true Jew is not one outwardly but one

inwardly, "and circumcision is circumcision of the heart, by the Spirit" (Rom. 2:29).

God's Revelation to Abraham

As compared with the earlier periods, during the time of Abraham, God revealed himself by speaking to him, but also by many more visible appearances. The common name for God was El Shaddai, which means the all-powerful one. From the Latin translation 'omnipotent' we get our English word 'Almighty'. It is interesting that El Shaddai is used so often in the part of Genesis dealing with Abraham's life, for so many things in his experience go contrary to nature. In no way could Abraham bring God's promises to realisation. They needed the almighty power of God himself. Thus when Abraham suggested that perhaps Ishmael could be considered the child of promise, he had to learn that a supernatural act was needed to achieve God's purpose (Gen. 17:17-19). Abraham, conscious of his own inability to fulfil what was spoken of in the promises, must have been greatly encouraged by all the teaching he was given of the character of El Shaddai.

During Abraham's life there were several appearances of the Angel of the Lord. These include the angel appearing to Hagar (Gen. 16:7-13), one of the three men who appeared to Abraham at Mamre (Gen. 18:1-33), and the angel who spoke to Abraham on Mount Moriah (Gen. 22:11-19). Later, the angel was to appear to Jacob, Moses, Balaam and others. The angel says he is God's messenger, but yet he made claims which only God could make. The appearances were a true revelation of God and specifically one in human form. The fullest expression of the idea behind these appearances came when Jesus was born. He was truly human as the son of Mary, yet truly God manifest in the flesh.

Abraham's Faith

Abraham's response to God's revelation was one of deep faith and intense spiritual vision. The epistle to the Hebrews highlights Abraham's faith and his response to the events in his life. He was a true pilgrim, who realised that his accommodation in Canaan was merely temporary, and therefore lived there like a stranger in a foreign land. He had been promised the land, but yet had to live in tents, and he had even to buy a burying place for his wife (Gen. 23). His real hope was set on something else, for he was looking for the city of the living God, that 'city with foundations whose builder and architect is God' (Heb. 11:9-10).

7

THE EXODUS

Israel in Egypt

The book of Genesis recounts the basic information about the lives of the patriarchs, Abraham, Isaac and Jacob. In making his covenant with Abraham, God had said that for 400 years Abraham's descendants would be enslaved in a foreign land until God punished their captors. Israel would then come out with many possessions (Gen. 15:13-14). The latter part of Genesis tells of how Jacob's favoured son, Joseph, was sold to Egypt, and how he was put in charge of the land (Gen. 41). Ultimately Jacob and his family joined Joseph and his wife and two sons in Egypt, making 70 persons in all (Gen. 46:26-27; Exod. 1:5. The figure of 75 in Acts 7:14 is taken from the Septuagint. It omitted Jacob and Joseph from the list, but included nine sons of Joseph).

The time spent by the Israelites in Egypt was 430 years (Exod. 12:40-41), and for the majority of that period we have no biblical commentary. The fewness in numbers of Israel when they first arrived in Egypt contrasts markedly with the large increase in size just before the Exodus (Exod. 1:6-22). God had fulfilled his first promise to Abraham and he had made his descendants into a great nation. The size of Israel presented a problem to the Egyptians,

41

especially if the Israelites ever sided with an invading army (Exod. 1:10). Hence they began to oppress them, and made them supply labour, including that needed for the building of the store cities of Pithom and Rameses. This oppression failed to reduce the numbers, and so the Hebrew midwives were instructed to kill all the Hebrew boys at birth. The manner in which the decree was evaded sets the background for the story of the birth and upbringing of Moses.

In their distress Israel had not been forsaken by God. They cried to him, and just as God had 'remembered' Noah because of his covenant (Gen. 8:1), so he 'remembered his covenant with Abraham, Isaac and Jacob' (Exod. 2:24; see also 3:16-17; 6:5). He was going to fulfil his promise of bringing them out of their slavery, and he would do so in a way which would reveal his grace and power.

The Call of Moses

Moses' parents trusted in the Lord, and they took steps to save their son. After being rescued from his basket in the reeds along the Nile, by God's providence his own mother was able to look after him until he became virtually an adopted son of Pharaoh's daughter (Exod. 2:1-11). While in Pharaoh's house he was educated in all the learning of the Egyptians and he became powerful in speech and action (Acts 7:22). At the age of forty he saw one of the Hebrew slaves being beaten. He intervened and killed the Egyptian, but when he

42

found out that his action was known to other Hebrews he fled to Midian. He thought that by his own power he could release his people from slavery. Instead he had to learn that deliverance would only come by the power of God (Acts 7:23-29).

Forty years later, while tending his father-in-law's flock, God appeared to him by means of the angel of the Lord (Exod. 3:1ff.) He saw a bush burning, but it was not burnt up. When he approached it, God spoke to him and several important truths were taught to him. Before he could act as God's servant to rescue his people he had to know

that God was holy. The angel of the Lord spoke to him as God himself, instructing him to take off his sandals because standing in God's presence he was on holy ground. He also hid his face, because he was frightened to look at this manifestation of God (Exod. 3:3,5-6).

that his God was the covenant God of his forefathers, Abraham, Isaac and Jacob. In making this declaration God referred back to the promise to Abraham concerning his people coming up out of the land of slavery (Exod. 3:6, 8, 17).

that this covenant God was to be known by a special name. It was so special that the Jews did not pronounce it. In our English Bibles it is printed as LORD. It appears also in an

Anglicised form as Jehovah or in its supposed original form as Yahweh. The name meant that he was the loving and gracious God who was going to show his nature in redeeming his covenant people.

that he was to be God's messenger, and the one through whom God would deliver his people. He had to speak God's word to both the Israelites and to Pharaoh. Moses was not an eloquent speaker, and therefore his brother Aaron acted as his spokesman (Exod. 4:10ff.)

that God would display his power against the Egyptians. God used a variety of words to describe his actions – redeem, deliver, bring out. All these terms emphasised that it was only God who could release the people from their bondage.

God's Deliverance
God's power was shown in so many ways to Israel and to the Egyptians. He performed miraculous signs for Moses (Exod. 4:1-9) and before Pharaoh (Exod. 7:6-13). He had assured Moses that he would strike the Egyptians with all his wonders (Exod. 3:20). This happened when he sent the ten plagues on Egypt, and they demonstrated his power over all of Egyptian life. The first nine all involved natural phenomena which God used in a supernatural way to bring judgement on the land.

This supernaturalness involved their severity, their coming in succession at Moses' command, and their unusual timing. They were also direct attacks on the religious life of Egypt, because the Egyptian gods were so bound up with the course of nature. The plagues were a judgement on the gods of Egypt (Exod. 12:12).

On the night of the last plague (the destruction of the first-born), the Israelites were finally commanded by Pharaoh to leave his country. God went ahead of them in the form of the pillar of cloud by day and the pillar of fire by night. When they were pursued by the Egyptians, both the angel of God and the pillar of cloud came round behind them and protected them (Exod. 14:19-20). The Egyptians were destroyed by the waters of the Red Sea, but the Israelites were saved by the Lord. This does not appear to have been the present Red Sea, but a considerable body of water further north, probably more in the area of the Bitter Lakes. The Hebrew text of the Old Testament refers to it as the Sea of Reeds. After their deliverance they sang the Song of Moses which commences: 'I will sing to the LORD, for he is highly exalted. The horse and its rider he has hurled into the sea. The LORD is my strength and my song; he has become my salvation' (Exod. 15:1-17).

The exodus was also a wonderful demonstration of God's grace. The difference between Egypt and Israel was not that one was better than the other. Instead, it was because God, having set his love on

Israel, had chosen them to be his people, and he had redeemed them from their slavery (Deut. 7:6-9). The institution of the Passover, with the sprinkling of the slain lamb's blood on the door frames, was to be an annual reminder of God's mercy in passing over or sparing the Israelites when he brought the tenth and final plague on the land. The great lesson was being taught by this ceremony that only through the shedding of blood was there forgiveness and acceptance by God. The Passover had much in common with the peace offerings, for it involved a communal meal as a symbol of the fellowship which the participants enjoyed with God. The Passover anticipated the far greater sacrifice of the Lamb of God who takes away the sin of the world (John 1:29). Jesus came as the final passover lamb when he offered up himself as a sacrifice for his people (1 Cor. 5:7).

8

THE COVENANT AT SINAI

The Position of Israel Before God

The making of the covenant on Mount Sinai came at a decisive point in Israel's history. Behind lay the exodus from Egypt and the experiences which the pilgrim people had been through as they moved down the peninsula to Sinai itself. This covenant marked a new stage in Israel's history, because it was a covenant with the nation, and not with individuals such as Noah or Abraham. It did not abolish what had been established by the earlier covenants but rather supplemented them (see Paul's words in Gal. 3:15ff.). The later historical songs incorporated in the Psalter make this plain (Pss. 105:8-12, 42-45; 106:45).

Just as the covenant was about to be made, God reminded Israel of all that had happened during the exodus. He declared: 'You have seen all that I did to the Egyptians, and how I bore you on eagles' wings and brought you to myself' (Exod. 19:4). He then called for their full obedience and observance of his covenant. After the regulations of the covenant were set out (Exod. 20-23), the people responded to the Lord and said: 'We will do everything the LORD has said; we will obey' (Exod. 24:7). God would keep his covenant even when his people were unfaithful, but to enjoy the blessings

47

of the covenant the obedience of the people was essential.

Out of all the nations God had chosen Israel, and this choice was to sonship. The relationship between God and Israel was unique. Pharaoh had been told: 'This is what the LORD says: Israel is my first-born son, and I told you, "Let my son go, so that he may worship me"' (Exod. 4:22-23). Exodus 19:3-6 sets out some of the important features of Israel's relationship with God. As a first-born son, Israel was in a position of special privilege and responsibility. God said that Israel was his treasured possession, and this same expression is repeated three times in Deuteronomy (7:6; 14:2; 26:18). In addition, Israel was to be 'a kingdom of priests' to God and 'a holy nation'. The first of these expressions suggests a worshipping and serving community, while the second reminds us that Israel as God's son had to reflect his character. They were to be holy, just as he was holy (Lev. 19:2). The language of Exodus 19 is taken over into the New Testament to describe the Christian church as 'a chosen people, a royal priesthood, a holy nation, a people belonging to God, that you may declare the praises of him who called you out of darkness into his wonderful light' (1 Pet. 2:9).

The Covenant Confirmed
On Mount Sinai God confirmed the covenants he had already made, and now added additional commitments for the people to observe. Once again

the emphasis is on God's initiative in dealing with his people. He called them to meet with him at Sinai, where he identified himself as the God who had redeemed them from the slavery of Egypt (Exod. 20:1-2). The circumstances of God's revelation of himself stressed both his majesty and power, and the solemnity of entering into a covenant with him (see the descriptions in Exod. 19:16ff.; 20:18-19; Deut. 5:22ff.). God chose to use a form of covenant well-known to the people of that day, having strong similarities to the Hittite treaties. After the demands of the covenant were set out in speech, the people responded and accepted the terms of the covenant placed on them. Then the representatives of Israel (Moses, Aaron, Nadab, Abihu and the 70 elders) went up to eat and drink on the mount of God (Exod. 24:9-11). This was a recognised way whereby people pledged themselves by an oath in a covenant setting.

At the centre of the requirements which God demanded of his people were the Ten Words (Exod. 34:28; Deut. 4:13; 10:4). Nowhere does the Bible tell us how the division into ten is to be made, and this explains why, for example, the Roman Catholic Church has a different division than Protestant churches have. They were written by God on two stone tablets, which are called in Deuteronomy 'the tablets of the covenant' (Deut. 9:9, 11, 15). The box or ark in which they were placed is called 'the ark of the covenant'. The Ten Words (translated very literally via Latin into English as 'the

Decalogue') contain the provisions for redeemed life under God's lordship. The actions of the people (their ethics) were determined by their religious commitment. Because they were God's covenant people, they were called to live in a distinctive way. All the Decalogue was devoted to duty towards God, even when actions and relationships with family and others were involved.

Very soon the people rebelled against God's covenant. While Moses was still up on the mount with God, under Aaron's leadership they made a golden calf. The people bowed down to it saying: 'These are your gods, O Israel, who brought you up out of Egypt' (Exod. 32:4, 8). At first God was going to destroy the people, but when Moses made intercession for the people on the basis of God's covenant with Abraham, Isaac and Jacob, God relented. On coming down from the mount, Moses broke the two stone tablets to show that the people had rebelled and broken God's covenant. New tablets were made, and God confirmed his covenant in a ceremony very similar to the one which had just taken place (Exod. 34; Deut. 9:7-21).

Life in God's Covenant
In addition to the Decalogue, many other laws were given by God. These related to various aspects of social life and behaviour, and they were intended to show how the nation, under God as its king, would organise its life. They are set out in the books of Exodus, Leviticus, Numbers and Deuteronomy.

As well as applying the basic principles of the Decalogue, these laws showed that Israel had to live in a distinctive manner. In matters of food and dress, for example, Israel was not to resemble the Canaanites, nor were they to try and find a message from the Lord by using heathen magic (Deut. 18:9ff.). God had spoken and his statutes stood firm. They were to be a lamp to the feet and a light to the path (Ps. 119:105).

Provision was especially made for worship, and these provisions were to last until the death of Jesus as the Messiah. Instructions were given concerning the building of the Tabernacle, with all its equipment and furniture. Each year had its special times when the people were to come together for the great festivals such as the Passover and the Feast of Tabernacles. Several important principles were brought out by these provisions. By means of the instruction given by priests and prophets Israel had to understand

that communal worship was to be at the place God appointed, notably at the Tabernacle. In a special way it symbolised God's presence with his people and his desire to draw near to them in his grace.

that sacrifice was an essential part of worship. They were taught that without the shedding of blood there could be no forgiveness of sins.

that more was required than just a formal offering of sacrifice. There had to be a humble and contrite heart in coming to seek God's face.

that the blood of bulls and goats could never take away sin. All the sacrifices were imperfect, and though using the sacrificial system, the people were taught to look for a day when God would finally remove sin. The New Testament shows us how this was fulfilled when Jesus offered himself as the great and final sacrifice for sin (Heb. 10:1-14).

9

WORSHIP IN ANCIENT ISRAEL

From the time of Moses worship in Israel took on new aspects, and because these are so important fuller comment on them is necessary. One very significant aspect was its corporate nature. No longer was it just a matter of families worshipping separately but provision was made for the assembly of the covenant people. From later references it is clear that the assembly or congregation was a standard feature of life in Israel (see Pss. 22:22, 25; 35:18; 40:9; 89:5; 107:32; 149:1; Joel 2:16; Mic. 1:5). The focal point of the assembly was the tabernacle, and it symbolised the central features of the relationship between God and his people. He dwelt among his people, and he spoke to them there. This fact is demonstrated very clearly in the provision of the temporary tent outside the camp of Israel when the covenant was broken at Sinai (Exod. 33:7-11). Once the covenant was renewed, the real tabernacle – the instructions concerning which had already been given (Exod. 25-27) – could now be built (Exod. 35-40).

The Tabernacle

Various names are used for the tabernacle. It is called 'the tent of meeting', the tabernacle', the sanctuary', and 'tent of testimony'. These names indicated different aspects of the function of the tabernacle. The first one indicates the idea of God's desire to come and draw near to his people. The word 'meeting' comes from a verb in Hebrew that has the idea of making an appointment. Israel met with God at the tabernacle by divine appointment. The word 'tabernacle' itself comes from a verb that means 'to dwell', so that it stresses the idea of God's abiding presence with his people. The term 'sanctuary' draws attention to God's holiness, while 'tent of testimony' showed that God's word had to be the guide for the lives of his people. Within the tabernacle was the ark of the covenant that contained the tablets of the covenant, while the book of the law (probably the whole of Deuteronomy) was placed beside it (Deut. 31:26).

In the time of Solomon the tabernacle (which was a movable tent) gave way to the more permanent structure of the temple. This temple, destroyed by the Babylonians in 586 BC, was rebuilt after the Exile and stood until destroyed by the Romans in 70 AD. When speaking with the Jews, Jesus indicated that the temple was giving way to the final and complete expression of God's presence in his own person (John 2:18-25), even though his own disciples could not understand this until after his resurrection. By taking on human flesh Jesus came to dwell with his people (John 1:14) and by his Spirit he still abides with them. Therefore the apostle John says: 'The tabernacle of God is with men' (Rev. 21:3).

Priests

While Moses at first served as a priest, he ceased to do so when he established the office of priesthood (Exod. 29:1) and ordained his brother Aaron as priest (Lev. 8:2-36). He had served as a priest on Mount Sinai (Exod. 22:3-8), supervising the work of the young men as they prepared the sacrifices. Later he also showed that the priest's work involved intercession, as he plead with God on behalf of the disobedient people (Exod. 32:11-13).

While the main function of the priest was to serve as a mediator between God and the people, it is clear that they had other roles as well. In some ways they acted like the prophets, just as Moses did after the incident of the golden calf in calling the people to repentance and submission. Part of their ministry was teaching the decrees that the Lord had given (Lev. 10:11). They may well, in addition to all the work involving sacrifices, have played an important role as resident and itinerant instructors in the law (see 2 Chron. 17:8-9; 19:8; Ezra 7:6; Jer. 18:18; Mal. 2:7).

No human priest is now required because Jesus made the perfect and final sacrifice of his own blood (Heb. 7:27; 9:28). He was both priest and sacrifice. All that the Old Testament priests did was ultimately fulfilled in Jesus our High Priest. He is very different from the priests in Israel because he is 'holy, blameless, pure, set apart from sinners, exalted above the heavens' (Heb. 7:26). In heaven he continues now as our intercessor.

The Ritual of Sacrifice

Many details about the sacrifices were specified for Israel by God. They were required because no one could come before God with their hands empty (Exod. 23:15; Deut. 16:16). Some of the sacrifices were blood offerings, dealing with the forgiveness of sins, while others called peace or fellowship offerings were eaten in a communal meal to show that fellowship with God had been restored. There were daily, weekly and annual offerings. Whatever was offered had to be the best. There should be no blemished offerings (Lev. 1:3; 3:1; Deut. 15:21, and repeated in many other places), though clearly at times the people infringed this rule (see Mal. 1:6-14).

The highlight of the whole system of sacrifices was the Day of Atonement (Lev. 16; *Yom Kippur*, as modern Jews still call it). On that day the high priest presented offerings for himself and for his family, before sacrificing two goats. One goat was slaughtered as a sin offering for the people and its blood taken beyond the curtain of the holy place and sprinkled on the cover of the ark. The other goat was taken away into the wilderness by the hand of some good man symbolically carrying away the sins of the people. While the first goat showed how forgiveness was obtained (by the shedding of blood) the second goat demonstrated the reality of forgiveness (sin is carried away as far as the east is from the west, Ps. 103:12).

Symbols and Types

The sacrifices of the Old Testament time were not *real* sacrifices. Just as the Lord's Supper does not have the real body and the real blood of Jesus, so the sacrifices were only symbols of great truths, and because they were symbols they could also serve to point forward to Jesus and his sacrifice. At the same time they could be symbols and also be types of Jesus.

A symbol is a thing or action that portrays in picture language some religious truth. That truth is a present reality at the time the symbol is employed. Thus for the Old Testament the slaying of an animal in sacrifice symbolised the truth that God would accept a substitute in place of a sinner. The symbols were of various kinds. There were those like the rainbow (Gen. 9:12-16) or the stairway at Bethel (Gen. 28:10-22, and compare John 1:50). Many of the symbols were connected with the sacrifices, or with the institutions of prophet, priest and king. Various events such as the Exodus also served to symbolise aspects of God's redemption.

Many of the symbols, though not all of them, pointed forward to an aspect of *the same truth* being pictured which would only come to pass in the time of the Messiah. While speaking of these truths to the people who used the symbols, they also served to point ahead as types of Jesus. They can therefore be described as acted-out prophecies concerning redemption. They were pictures of what God would do through the coming of Jesus. The diagram below sets out this relationship using the Day of Atonement as an example, and shows how things in the Old Testament could be both symbols and types:

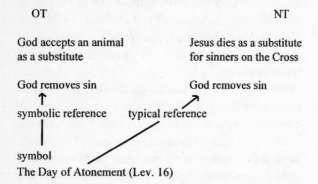

OT   NT

God accepts an animal   Jesus dies as a substitute
as a substitute   for sinners on the Cross

God removes sin   God removes sin

symbolic reference   typical reference

symbol
The Day of Atonement (Lev. 16)

How could people in the Old Testament realise that something was pointing to Jesus? The very fact that the sacrifices were so imperfect and needed repetition must have awakened in many the realisation that they were pointing to something fuller and better. Also, we must think of the role of prophets and priests as teachers. Just as we have preaching to instruct us about the significance of Jesus' death as symbolised in the Lord's Supper, so at that time the people had teachers to help them understand the meaning of the sacrificial system. The prophets taught that God's servant, the Messiah, would be put to death in order to take away our iniquities (Isa. 53), and that in one dramatic day a fountain would be opened for sin and uncleanness (Zech. 13:1).

10

THE CONQUEST AND THE
PERIOD OF THE JUDGES

The Wilderness Wanderings

Just over a year after the Exodus from Egypt the children of Israel left Sinai and moved north until they were on the southern edge of the land of Canaan. The fullest account of their movements in the period between leaving Sinai and finally entering Canaan is given in Numbers 10:11-36:13, with a summary statement in Deuteronomy 1:1-3:11. From Kadesh Barnea spies were sent out to investigate the land promised to them. The twelve spies all reported that the land was exceedingly fruitful, but that it was occupied by groups of strong and powerful people. Of all the spies Caleb encouraged the people to go in and take possession of the land (Num. 13:30-33), and in this he was joined by Joshua (Num. 14:6-9). They knew that the Lord was going to lead them into the land and protect them. The people as a whole rebelled against the Lord, at first refusing to enter Canaan, and then sinfully going in without Moses or the presence of the Ark of the Covenant (Num. 14:41-45). They were defeated and then they had to spend 38 years wandering in the wilderness before they entered Canaan from the east.

After those years in the desert, the Israelites

moved first to the east and then to the north of the Dead Sea, crossing the territories of Edom and Moab, before defeating the Amorite kings, Sihon of Heshbon and Og of Bashan. The captured territories were allotted to the tribes of Reuben and Gad, with half the tribe of Manasseh also receiving its territory. When the Israelites came to the plains of Moab on the east bank of the Jordan, Moses had to hand over the leadership to Joshua. God had told him earlier that because he did not trust the Lord wholly, he was not to lead the people into the promised land (Num. 20:12). Instead Joshua was to assume the leadership, and he would bring them into possession of the land promised long before to Abraham.

The Covenant Renewed

Before entering Canaan, the covenant with the Lord was renewed. Such a covenant renewal was common in the secular world of the day. Slight alterations of the requirements were also made at such a ceremony. The Book of Deuteronomy as a whole forms a document detailing the covenant renewal in the Plains of Moab. After reminding the people of their recent history (chaps. 1-4), Moses again set out the Ten Words. There were slight changes to them to take account of the new situation (see Deut. 5:12-15, 21 as cf. with Exod. 20:8-11, 17). Following this proclamation of God's demands, Moses expounded the significance of the Ten Words (Deut. 6-26), before making formal provision for Joshua to take over from him and for the covenant requirements to be taught to succeeding generations. At the end of the book of Deuteronomy, when we read of Moses' death and burial (Deut. 34), Israel had not yet come into possession of the promised land. The five books of Moses (often called the Pentateuch) end with the promises to Abraham only partially fulfilled.

The Conquest

The basic theme of the book of Joshua is the fulfilment of God's covenant promises concerning the land. This is emphasised by the accounts at the end of the book of the burial of Joshua, Eleazar and Joseph (Jos. 24:29-33). These men were all buried in the land which belonged to Israel, in contrast to Abraham who had to bargain for a burying place for his wife (Gen. 23:1-20).

The account of the conquest in Joshua has two aspects to it. On the one hand, the stress is on the fulfilment of God's promises concerning the land (see 11:23; 14:13-15; 21:43-45). They achieved possession of the land from the desert in the south to Lebanon in the north, from the Great Sea (the Mediterranean) to the river Euphrates in the east (Josh. 1:4). On the other hand, the unfinished nature of the conquest is also made plain, for strong pockets of Canaanites still remained (Josh. 13:13; 15:63; 16:10; 17:12-13; 23:4-5). The opening chapter of the book of Judges endorses these same aspects.

The conquest proceeded in several stages. The

first thing needed was to cross the Jordan and to capture Jericho. The men of the two and a half tribes who already had their territory had to leave their families and possessions and take part in the battles ahead. God intervened in a miraculous way to permit the crossing of the Jordan, even though it was at flood level (Jos. 3:9-17). Jericho fell before the armies of the Lord, again with miraculous help. Joshua was acting on the instructions of the captain of the Lord's army when he gave his orders to the people (Jos. 5:13-6:27). The city and its inhabitants were destroyed, except for Rahab the harlot and her family, for she had hidden the spies who first came into the city (Josh. 2). When the city was destroyed a curse was placed upon the man who undertook to rebuild it. That curse came to fulfilment when in King Ahab's time a man called Hiel rebuilt Jericho (1 Kings 16:34). From Jericho the central uplands were captured, before a southern campaign enabled Joshua to take all the territory down to and including the Negev (Josh. 10:29-43). Then the northern part of the country was taken right up to the region of Mount Hermon (Josh. 11).

The Judges – Preparation for Kingship
The period of Israel's history in which there was rule by judges is covered in the books of Judges, Ruth and the early part of 1 Samuel. The theology of this period is summarised in Judges 2. That chapter opens with a reference to the covenant oath regarding the land, and to the fact that Israel had

already broken specific covenant provisions (vv. 2-3, cf. v. 20). As part of the penalty God was to leave the Canaanites to be a snare to them and as a means of testing them (vv. 3, 22). In their distress the Israelites cried to God and he saved them by raising up a deliverer or saviour. The accounts of men like Gideon and Samson are really records of how God saved his people by his chosen servants. The biblical text does not extol men like these as national heroes, but rather as instruments in God's hand to provide salvation for his people. In Judges there is a whole series of incidents which show the same pattern. The people cry to God in their distress, he provides help, and then there is further unfaithfulness on the part of the people.

When they were settled in the land two dangers faced Israel. From within, the faith of the Canaanites threatened Israel's commitment to the Lord, while from without, Israel's security was threatened by attacks from surrounding nations. Without an institution like the later synagogue, the means of instructing the people were limited and not well organised. Superficial similarities between Israel's faith and that of the Canaanites (such as sacrifice, sanctuaries, altars, the use of the term Baal) must have attracted many. Israel had to ward off external attacks from neighbours like the Moabites, Midianites and especially the Philistines. By the end of the time of the Judges there was very real danger to Israel because of confrontation with the Philistines to the north, west and south.

Towards the end of the period covered by the book of Judges, various problems were present in Israel, notably religious (ch. 17), political (ch. 18), and moral ones (ch. 19). The people were clearly dissatisfied, especially with the political situation. Three times the author of Judges expresses it in this way: 'In those days Israel had no king; everyone did what was right in his own eyes' (17:6; 18:1; 19:1). The same statement is used to end the whole book (21:25). This meant that everyone was his own king. The book of Judges graphically illustrates what this entailed for Israel. An invitation was given to Gideon to become king (8:22-23) but he rejected it. Their experiences of being their own kings made the people all the more ready to look for a king of God's appointment.

11

THE INTRODUCTION OF KINGSHIP

Preparation for Kingship

In the period of the patriarchs God had indicated
that in time to come kings would be functioning in
Israel. He promised Abraham that kings would
come forth from him (Gen. 17:16), while Jacob, on
his return from Mesopotamia, was given a similar
promise (Gen. 35:11). At the end of the Song of
Moses the people sang: 'The LORD will reign for
ever and ever' (Exod. 15:18). However, Moses gave
explicit instructions concerning the kingship which
God would eventually institute in Israel. The future
introduction of kingship was clearly in God's
purposes, and Moses set out the character and
conduct of the king who should be appointed over
Israel (Deut. 17:14ff.). Clearly the prevailing
practices of Near Eastern monarchs were something
to be avoided by Israel. The most important
requirements were that the king could not be a
foreigner but had to be an Israelite (as with the
prophets, cf. Deut. 18:15) and that he had to direct
his own life by the copy of God's law he was to
own. The covenant document was to be the king's
guide so that he could direct the affairs of the nation
in true dependence upon the Lord.

The introduction of kingship into Israel had to
wait for several centuries after the conquest of

Canaan. During the intervening period Israel was ruled by judges. The book of Judges describes what life was like without the monarchy. The problems which Israel experienced in the absence of a king are illustrated by all the accounts of incidents during this period. These experiences made the people more ready to look for a king and a hereditary royal family. The last of the judges was Samuel, whose judgeship overlaps in time with the latter period recorded in the book of Judges. He is specifically called a judge (1 Sam. 7:15-17), but he was more than that. He was also a prophet, being recognised as one from Dan in the north to Beersheba in the south (1 Sam. 3:20). In addition, he was also a priest (1 Sam. 9:12-13; 13:8-13).

The Request for a King
1 Samuel 8 records the visit of the elders of Israel to Samuel. They requested him to appoint a king over them. The aged Samuel reacted bitterly to the request. He took it as a personal insult, and certainly later he set out to defend his own character (1 Sam. 12:1-5). However, the Lord made it plain to him that the people had not rejected Samuel but rather that by their actions they had rejected the Lord himself. In part Samuel's response was not in keeping with God's intentions for his people. There was nothing intrinsically wrong with the request of the elders. The difficulty lay in their motives and manner, rather than in the fact of the request itself. The elders wanted a king

because they had reason to fear that Samuel's sons would succeed their father. Joel and Abijah were acting as judges at Beersheba in the south, while Samuel confined himself to a relatively small circuit in the area just north of Jerusalem. Those sons were not following in the ways of their father, and they were perverting the course of justice (1 Sam. 8:1-3).

because the people sensed their own insecurity. They specifically referred to the fact that they wanted a king to go and lead them in their battles (1 Sam. 8:19-20). Later, Samuel also mentioned this reason to them (1 Sam. 12:12). This insecurity really stemmed from their own lack of faith in the Lord. When Nahash king of the Ammonites came against Israel, the people should have sought God's help and prayed for him to raise up a leader. Instead, they wanted the appointment of a king whom they thought would be able to save them.

because they were not willing to wait for God's time, and so were prepared to break their covenant commitments. The timing and manner of the request was incompatible with the covenant relationship, and the consequence of their action was a breach of the covenant (1 Sam. 8:7; 10:19).

God's response was one of mercy. They were in great need, and just as God had looked upon his people in need in Egypt (Exod. 2:25; 3:7-9), so he looked on them again and provided a deliverer (1 Sam. 9:16). Saul was the chosen king, and Samuel gathered all the people together at Mizpah and declared to them the law of the king (1 Sam. 10:17-25). The purpose of this declaration was doubtless to set out the role of the king both for the benefit of the people and the king-designate.

The Chosen King
The choice of Saul was God's immediate answer to the request of Israel. Physically he was outstanding among the people (1 Sam. 10:23-24), and when he was presented to the people by Samuel, they all shouted, 'Long live the king!' When Nahash the Ammonite besieged Jabesh-Gilead (east of the Jordan), Saul led out his men and routed the attackers (1 Sam. 11:1-11). Immediately after this battle Samuel called all the people to assemble at Gilgal, and there they renewed their allegiance to the kingdom of the Lord. In effect this was a covenant renewal ceremony, like that conducted by Moses in the plains of Moab (Deut. 29ff.), or that by Joshua at Shechem (Jos. 8:30-35; 24:1-27). In many ways Saul had more in common with the preceding judges than he had with the later kings of Israel. For example, he exhibited the charisma typical of the judges (1 Sam. 10:23-24; 11:5-15). However, in his personal life Saul lacked self-

control, and at heart he was rebellious against God. In spite of military successes he was twice rejected by the Lord, seemingly at an interval of about twenty years (1 Sam. 13-14; 15). In addition to the experience of the judges, Israel had now had further preparation for true kingship by having the wrong kind of king.

David's Kingship
God's ultimate choice for the people was the man after his own heart, David (1 Sam. 13:14). Samuel was sent by God to Bethlehem to anoint one of Jesse's sons as king (1 Sam. 16:1-13). From that point onwards the narrative in the books of Samuel concentrates on David rather than Saul. There was a long period of hostility between them, before the ultimate death of Saul on the mountains of Gilboa (to the south-west of the Sea of Galilee). David had the opportunity to kill Saul, but he refused to take the life of the one who was God's anointed (1 Sam. 24:4-6; 26:8-11). The men of Judah anointed David as king at Hebron (2 Sam. 2:2-4), to be followed by a later anointing there by the men of Israel (2 Sam. 5:1-5).

In many ways David was no better than Saul, for he was a murderer and an adulterer. However, the Old Testament tells us that in other respects he was far superior. David was able to

stabilise the whole national life of Israel, probably with the help of the able men who had gathered round him when he was fleeing from Saul. He had been joined at the cave of Adullam by a group of 400 men, and the presence of so many discontents may well point to deep economic and social problems during the reign of Saul (1 Sam. 22:1-2).

remove the threat of the Philistines, and to conquer the last areas of Canaanite influence. Under David and his son Solomon the promised limits of the land were realised (1 Kings 4:21,24).

establish a dynasty which was going to endure, and from which in the fullness of time Jesus would come. God promised him a dynasty, and when he spoke through prophets such as Isaiah of the coming Messiah, the announcement was in terms of this covenant with David (2 Sam. 7:1-16; Isa. 9:6-7). When Gabriel told Mary that she was going to give birth to Jesus, he said he would sit on David's throne and reign for ever and ever (Luke 1:30-33). At the very end of the New Testament Jesus says: 'I am the Root and the Offspring of David, and the bright Morning Star' (Rev. 22:16).

12

THE FATE OF THE MONARCHY

The Transition to Solomon
David clearly intended that Solomon should be his
successor. He had made an oath to this effect, but
Bathsheba had to remind him of this when Adonijah
decided to seize the kingship for himself (1 Kings
1:5-10, 17-21). Nathan the prophet knew of the oath,
and he, Zadok the priest, and Benaiah the army
commander combined in taking Solomon to Gihon
and anointing him as king (1 Kings 1:38-40). When
David died, Solomon immediately took over as
king, though he acted in a ruthless and bloodthirsty
manner in getting rid of his opposition. The period
of David was the high point in the history of Israel,
and in the covenant God made with him (2 Sam. 7)
the Messianic concept came to be stated in terms
of Davidic kingship. David's kingship was
thereafter regarded as the standard by which all
other reigns were judged. However, the succeeding
history showed there was tension between the vision
set for Israel, and the reality of what actually
transpired.

Solomon's Reign
Things seemed so promising at the start of
Solomon's reign. He had received excellent advice
from his father (1 Kings 2:1-9), and at Gibeon had

71

pleased God with his request for wisdom (1 Kings 3:4-15). His main aim was to preserve and consolidate the gains made under David. There was a glory about Solomon's kingdom (cf. Jesus' words in Matt. 6:29). He reorganised the administrative structure of the kingdom, which now had twelve districts, each of which was to support the royal court for a month at a time. The army was also reorganised and strengthened, while a major building programme was carried out. The plans and preparations for building the Temple had been made by David, but it was Solomon who brought it to reality (1 Kings 5-8). It was not meant to be for the greater glory of Solomon, but as a witness to the world that the God of Israel was the God over all (see 1 Chron. 22:5). Other building programmes by Solomon included his own palace, and the strongly fortified cities of Hazor, Megiddo and Gezer (1 Kings 9:10-23).

Other aspects of Solomon's reign were not praiseworthy. His building programme placed stress on the country as a whole, for taxation had to pay for it. In addition, he had to conscript people to work on these projects. His own throne was most elaborate, quite unlike any other one known (1 Kings 10:20). His most serious sins, however, involved his numerous marriages, including one to the daughter of the Egyptian Pharaoh. As he grew older these wives led him into heathen worship, and he even built places of worship for Chemosh, the god of the Moabites, and for Molech, the god of the Ammonites (1 Kings 11:7-8). Outwardly his kingdom seemed to bring to fulfilment the promises to Abraham, but yet it was marred by his own sinfulness. He was warned by God that after his death the kingdom would be divided, with just one tribe (Judah) left for the sake of David, God's servant (1 Kings 11:11-13). When Jeroboam, a northerner, who was in charge of the labour force for the families of Joseph, rebelled against Solomon, Ahijah the prophet repeated the warning which God had already given to Solomon (1 Kings 11:29-40). Because Solomon was trying to kill him, Jeroboam fled to Egypt and stayed there till Solomon's death.

The Division of the Kingdom
The faults made by Solomon were serious in themselves, but they were aggravated by other factors as well. There was a long-standing jealousy between Judah and the Joseph tribes, Ephraim and Manasseh. Joseph had been given the right of the first-born in place of Reuben, and the privileged position was emphasised in Jacob's blessing (Gen. 49: 22-26). Incidents such as the one concerning Achan (Jos. 7:1), who was from Judah, allowed a separation to develop between the northern tribes and Judah in the south. When Saul died David was anointed as king over Judah at Hebron (2 Sam. 2:4), but it was seven and a half years later before he was acknowledged as king over Israel (2 Sam. 5:1-5). That the kingdom was never fully integrated under David's rule is shown by the two rebellions

which took place under him (see 2 Sam. 15:1-12; 20:1-26).

On the death of Solomon, Jeroboam immediately returned from Egypt and led the northern tribes in seeking an easier time under Solomon's son, Rehoboam. Acting on the advice of his young friends, and against the advice of the elders, Rehoboam threatened even harsher treatment. Immediately the northern tribes responded: 'What share do we have in David, what part in Jesse's son? To your tents, O Israel! Look after your own house, O David!' (1 Kings 12:16; and compare the similar words used earlier by Sheba, 2 Sam. 20:1). They then went to their homes, and a short time later at a formal assembly Jeroboam was appointed as king over Israel (1 Kings 12:20). Ahijah's prophecy was fulfilled, and only the tribe of Judah remained loyal to David's family.[1]

Clearly, then, a combination of factors played their part in the division. Jealousy of Judah was very real, for the northern tribes knew that God had 'rejected the tents of Joseph', and that 'he did not choose the tribe of Ephraim; but he chose the tribe of Judah, Mount Zion, which he loved' (Ps. 78:67-

---

1. The tribe of Simeon had never had a unified territorial area (see Josh. 19:1-9) and it appears to have been incorporated into Judah by the time of David (2 Chr. 4:24-43). The ten northern tribes included the two Joseph tribes (Ephraim and Manasseh) and Benjamin (Ps. 80:1-2) but excluded the tribe of Levi, because it had no tribal territory.

68). The burdens of the new monarchy created a groundswell of unrest, while Solomon's sins brought God's judgment on the kingdom. God tore Israel from the house of David (2 Kings 17:21).

The Divided Monarchy

From the time the division in the kingdom came in 931 BC, the northern kingdom had an independent existence until it fell to the Assyrians in 722 BC. The southern kingdom of Judah lasted for another 140 years, until it fell when Jerusalem was finally destroyed by the Babylonians in 586 BC. After concentrating on David (and to a lesser extent on Solomon), the writers of the history of Israel and Judah in the books of Kings give a skeletal account of the history down to the fall of Jerusalem. No attempt is made to give a detailed account of each king's reign, but information is given as to where additional information can be found regarding it ('the annals of the kings of Israel', 'the annals of the kings of Judah'). What creates difficulty for the modern reader is that there was clearly an intention to keep a unified picture of Israel and Judah within a particular time frame. This results in the vision of the historical writer(s) switching backwards and forwards from Israel to Judah. The books of Chronicles do not give any account of the history of Israel, and even seem to deliberately avoid mention of it.

The Rebelliousness of Israel

Right from the outset, Israel went its own way in religious matters. Because Jeroboam did not want his people going to Jerusalem to worship, he set up golden calves at Bethel and Dan. In addition, he built shrines on Canaanite high places and appointed people to minister there, even though they were not from priestly families (1 Kings 12:31). The succeeding kings of Israel were like Jeroboam, and the usual comment on them is that they 'did not turn from the sins of Jeroboam' (as an example see the comment on Joram, 2 Kings 3:1-3). There was no hereditary royal family in the northern kingdom and many of the kings died violently.

But God had not forsaken the people in Israel. Just as there were earlier prophets such as Nathan, Ahijah, and Shemaiah, major prophets such as Elijah and Elisha appear on the scene. Around 750 BC two prophets were speaking God's word to the northern kingdom (Hosea and Amos), while two others (Isaiah and Micah) were prophesying to both kingdoms. God was going to judge Israel, yet his people in Judah were not going to escape his judgment either (Amos 2:4 - 3:15). Promises were given that a people whom God could refer to as 'Not Loved' (*Lo-Ruhamah*) and 'Not My People' (*Lo-Ammi*) would ultimately be called 'sons of the living God' (Hosea 1:6-11, and see the quotation of this passage in Romans 9:25-26).

13

THE PROPHETS

Messages from the Lord

Throughout the earlier part of Old Testament history
God spoke to his people Israel, using individuals
like Abraham or Moses as his means of
communication with his people. Moses was
especially favoured because the Lord spoke to him
face to face, whereas other prophets did not have
this closeness of fellowship (Num. 12:6-8). Because
at times God used means like visions, the word used
for the spokesman from God was at first 'seer' (1
Sam. 9:9). This word and another similar one
emphasised the manner in which they received the
message from God. However, the most frequent
term for the spokesman came to be 'prophet'. Just
as Aaron was Moses' 'prophet' (Exod. 4:16; 7:1-
2), so God used a succession of messengers called
'prophets' to speak his word to Israel and Judah.

When Israel was about to enter into the land of
Canaan, in addition to making provision for kings
in Israel (Deut. 17:14-20), Moses also gave God's
direction concerning how the people were to receive
his messages. As soon as they came into the land
they would be confronted with various Canaanitish
practices. These practices were detestable to God,
and Israel was instructed not to try and imitate them.
Nine of these practices involving witchcraft and

sorcery were set out (Deut. 18:9-13). Instead, Israel was to be blameless before the Lord, and he promised that he would give them a prophet who would declare his word. The prophet was to be

like Moses and to act as a spokesman for the Lord to the people.

from among the Israelites, and not a foreigner. While a man like Balaam could be hired to speak God's message, yet he could never occupy the office of prophet (Num. 22–24).

a person in whose mouth God would put words and he would then speak them in God's name.

a permanent institution in Israel to protect the Israelites and to ensure that further teaching would be given of the basic covenant concepts.

The passage in Deuteronomy tells of a long line of prophets. God was going to send the prophets as his messengers to speak to Israel. However, ultimately the promise concerning the prophet was to find its fulfilment in the person of Jesus. The institution of a line of prophets was going to serve the people well, but its intention was also to point them forward to the coming of the great and final prophet. The New Testament tells us that this message in Deuteronomy found its fulfilment in the person of Jesus (Acts 3:22-23; 7:37).

The Task of the Prophets

The major task of the prophet was to be a spokesman for God. This involved proclaiming God's word to his own generation (forth-telling) as well as sometimes announcing God's word concerning the future (fore-telling). The initial calls of both Isaiah (Isa. 6:1-8) and Jeremiah (Jer. 1:4-10) illustrate this role. In both cases their lips were touched, indicating the need for cleansing and for God's grace if they were to proclaim his message (see Isa. 6:7; Jer. 1:9). When God called a prophet he commissioned him to go and say: 'This is what the Lord says.' This is illustrated, for example, by the words of the Lord to Amos when he was called to become a prophet (Amos 7:14-16).

Another task of the prophets was to guard the kingdom of God. They were not appointed to introduce new laws. Rather, they had to enforce the laws given through Moses long before. Thus, the last of the Old Testament prophets, Malachi, appeals to the law of Moses as the basis for the life of the people as he ends his book (Mal. 4:4). The office of the prophet was needed to keep Israel in a true covenant relationship with God. Often the kings tried to find political solutions to problems, while the prophets urged the people to seek the Lord and to find his will for them. Inevitably, the relationship between prophets and kings was not always good, and the prophets could never accept the separation of religion from politics. One of the terms used for the prophets ('watchmen') emphasised this task of guarding the life of the nation (see Jer. 6:17; Ezek. 3:17; 33:7).

The third great task of the prophets was to write down the history of Israel and Judah. The books like Joshua, Judges, 1 and 2 Samuel, and 1 and 2 Kings, which we regard as historical books, are called 'the former prophets' by the Jewish people. The 'latter prophets' comprise Isaiah, Jeremiah, Ezekiel, and the twelve minor prophets. They called the historical books by this title because they regarded them as coming from the prophets and as being written from the perspective of the prophets. Thus the historical books are interested in more than just a mere recital of facts. Often they comment on the events they are recording and pass judgements on persons and incidents.

The Periods of Prophetic Activity
Although Abraham was a prophet (Gen. 20:7), and the patriarchs were in general considered to be prophets (Ps. 105:15), yet the office of prophet only came to the fore in the period marking the commencement of kingship in Israel. Hence there was a close relationship between the institutions of prophecy and kingship. The role of the prophets differed somewhat in the later stages of Old Testament history as compared with the earlier period. From Samuel down to the series of prophets in the 8th century BC (Hosea, Micah, Amos and Isaiah), there was stress on the spoken word of the Lord through his servants the prophets. The majority

of these spoken messages are not recorded in the Bible, as God did not require them to be written and preserved for later generations. There are accounts of the ministries of important prophets such as Elijah and Elisha, and there are also some small prophecies by other prophets embedded in the historical books (e.g. the words of the unnamed prophet who spoke about the birth of Josiah, 1 Kings 13:1-3). The activity of various other prophets are mentioned without any extensive record of their actual words. From the middle of the 8th century BC down to the end of Old Testament history there was not only oral proclamation but written prophecies. These prophecies were addressed to the northern kingdom of Israel (and the re-united Israel after the Exile), the southern kingdom of Judah, and the Gentile nations like Nineveh and Edom (cf. Nahum and Obadiah). The prophets were also during this period the recorders of the history of Israel and Judah, and in so doing often passed judgements on the events they recounted. David is often given as the model king, and others were judged by the standard of his devotion to the Lord (see for an example 1 Kings 15:1-5 regarding Abijah).

In the earlier part of this prophetic history, the stress was more on the need for repentance towards God. However, while the later prophets do not neglect this call, yet they placed the stress on the vision of what God was going to do 'in the last days'. This expression, like other similar ones, takes on the meaning of the glorious Messianic day when God would not just repair the situation of his people but do something altogether new. In that great day the sin of the people would be removed by God. Repeatedly the people were told by the prophets that God was not satisfied with sheer formality of worship, but that he desired a vital relationship with them. Such a relationship was to be expressed also in concern for the poor and the needy, and in seeing that justice was duly administered. Commitment to God, asserted the prophets, brought with it the responsibility to live according to the demands of God's law. A redeemed people had to act justly, love mercy, and walk humbly with their God (Mic. 6:8).

14

POETS AND WISE MEN

Hebrew Poetry

The poetry of the Old Testament is typical for the Middle Eastern region. As such, it is very different from English and other Western poetry. We depend mainly upon rhythm (a set number of syllables per line) and rhyme (the use of the same sounds at the ends of lines). These do not feature strongly in Hebrew poetry. Instead, Hebrew poetry depends upon features such as

the extensive use of what is called parallelism. This means that after stating an idea either the opposite may be expressed (see Ps. 1:6) or perhaps the same idea is given in different words (see Ps. 24:1). At other times there is the addition of complementary ideas which lead to a climax (see Ps. 29:1).

the use of acrostics, of which Psalm 119 is the fullest. In this psalm there are twenty-two sections, following the letters of the Hebrew alphabet. In each section every verse begins with the appropriate letter of the alphabet. This distinctive feature cannot be preserved in translation into English. Other examples can be found in Psalms 9-10, 25, 34, 111-112, and Lamentations 1-3.

the copious use of various literary features, some of which, like alliteration and assonance, are used to a much greater degree than in Western poetry.

The Psalms

One of the ways in which we respond to God's goodness and grace is by singing. While there are important songs recorded throughout the Old Testament (e.g. the Song of Moses, Exod. 15:1-18; the song of Deborah and Barak, Judg. 5:1-31; Hannah's song, 1 Sam. 2:1-10), yet the majority are in a single collection called in Hebrew, 'Praises'. Our English word 'Psalms' comes from a Greek word meaning 'songs'. This collection of 150 songs was finalised after the return from Exile in Babylon, as is shown by the presence of songs such as Psalm 137 ('By the waters of Babylon we sat and wept') and Psalm 126 ('When the LORD restored the captives of Zion'). The earliest song in the collection is one attributed to Moses (Psalm 90). The Psalter represents, therefore, centuries of praises in Israel.

Clearly those who put the Psalter together as a collection (probably Ezra and his associates after the return from Exile) did so with deliberate design. Indications of the planning behind the present structure of the Psalter include

the division of it into five books (Psalms 1-41; 42-72; 73-89; 90-106; 107-150), with a doxology at the end of each section.

the grouping together of psalms by particular composers (e.g. psalms of David, principally in Psalms 2-41, 51-71, 138-145; psalms of Asaph, Psalms 50, 73-83; psalms of the sons of Korah, Psalms 42, 44-49, 84, 85, 87, 88).

the deliberate linking together of psalms with similar themes (e.g. Psalms 23-24; 42-43), or those with similar titles such as the Songs of Ascent (Psalms 120-134).

There are not many indications within the Old Testament of how the Psalms were used nor of the manner in which they were brought together to form a single collection. Reference is made in 1 Chronicles 16:8-36, Ezra 3:10-11, and Jeremiah 33:11 to the use of some parts of the Psalter. Clearly, at times words were taken from several psalms and combined together as a suitable offering of praise to God.

The Psalms tell us a great deal about the way in which Old Testament believers praised God for who he was, and prayed to him as the saviour of his people. Constantly they direct attention to the character of God, who stands in his majesty and holiness over against frail and sinful man. When man is in view, the great distinction is between the righteous and the wicked (see Psalm 1 for an excellent illustration). A living connection with the God of the covenant did not flow from human achievement but solely because of divine grace. Those who lack this living relationship with him show this by a life of systematic evil-doing. They are violent, arrogant, flattering, and plot against the righteous. They are devoid of the fear of the Lord which is the beginning of wisdom (Ps. 111:10).

The Wise Men and their Writings
Within the Old Testament there is reference to a group of men called 'the wise', and various parts of the Old Testament, principally the books of Job, Proverbs, Ecclesiastes, and Song of Solomon, have been called 'the Wisdom books'. The wisdom spoken of in the Old Testament is presented as a gift of God, but also as wisdom which demands a response from believers. They respond with fear or reverence for God, and no term is more expressive of true love and devotion to God than this. God's wisdom is not merely theoretical but intensely practical, as it forms the foundation of all our conduct. Earlier in the Old Testament men such as Abraham and Joseph demonstrated the fear of God, just as the people of Israel as a whole did so at the time of the Exodus (Exod. 14:31). The book of Deuteronomy emphasises that this fear is a result of hearing and responding to God's word (Deut. 4:10; 8:6). Solomon later prayed at the dedication of the Temple in Jerusalem for all the peoples of the earth that they might know God's name and fear him (1 Kings 8:43). It is especially in some of the Psalms and in the books of Proverbs, Ecclesiastes and Job that the concept of the fear of the Lord is so central.

The wisdom books of the Old Testament differ from one another in style, but they are all directed to the same practical end.

Job tells of an historical figure who lived in the desert east of Palestine. After the introduction (chapters 1-2) there are three cycles of speeches by Job's three friends, who argue that Job must have sinned to be suffering as he is (chapters 3-31). Job responds to each cycle of accusations and turns to God in complaint and petition. Then Elihu enters and takes issue with them and with Job (chapters 32-37). At last God speaks and shows Job how man's knowledge is limited. It is God who works his sovereign will, and his dealings show that he 'is full of compassion and is merciful' (James 5:11).

Proverbs is just what the name suggests – a collection of short, pithy statements. Proverbs in almost all languages are brief, are concrete not abstract, state a general truth, and often have diverse applications. The teaching of the book of Proverbs sets God's wisdom against the philosophies of the world. Fear of God is the first principle of life, and those in a right relationship with God are in a position to understand the world around them.

Ecclesiastes presents a mirror for man, so that he can see how transient is all his work. It is only God's work which endures. The key to the book is probably the exhortation in the final chapter to seek God while one is young, so that life can be seen from a proper perspective (Eccles. 12:1-14).

Song of Solomon is in the first instance concerned with human love and the human marriage relationship. The book constitutes powerful preaching concerning pure and true married love, which God himself has bestowed as his gift (see 8:6, love 'burns like a blazing fire, like the very flame of the LORD', NIV margin). The marriage relationship is used in both Old and New Testaments to point to the loving relationship between God and his people (Hos. 1-3; Jer. 2:2; 3:14; Eph. 5:22ff.).

The fear of the Lord and its practical out-working in life is the dominating idea of the Wisdom books. Not only was it the response of faith to God, but it also provided an understanding of men and society that gave cohesion and purpose to all aspects of human life. Without the fear of the Lord, life has no satisfaction, and in the end it becomes utterly meaningless.

15

UNVEILING THE FUTURE

Prophecy

While the prophet's role was to minister God's word to his own generation, yet from its outset the institution of prophecy was concerned with prediction of the future. In Deuteronomy 18, this aspect of prophecy was expressly mentioned. Moses depicts time in the future when the people would want to know how to distinguish between true and false prophecy. They were to be told that a false prophet's predictions would not come to pass. Such a prophet had spoken presumptuously and without divine authorisation (Deut. 18:21-22). This type of prediction by the prophets was not necessarily to be equated with pre-written history. That is to say, when the prophets spoke of the future they did not do so in a way similar to the form of narrative used by the historical writers to record what actually happened in the history of Israel. Various factors in prophecy highlight these differences between history and prophecy, between narrative and prediction. These features are not peculiar to the Old Testament prophets, but can be seen in the prophetic ministry of Jesus (see Matt. 24-25, Mark 13) or in the book of Revelation.

Prophecy contains many of the figures of speech which are characteristic of poetry. Thus the prophets used language which was not meant to be taken literally, but which, because of its graphic imagery, pressed home the real meaning of the message (cf. Isaiah's descriptions of the coming of the Assyrians in chapters 7 and 8 of his prophecy).

In the Bible, prophecy is a wonderful combination of what is clear with what is very obscure. Enough is told in plain language of God's purposes to arouse expectation concerning the fulfilment of the prophecies, while so many of the actual details are deliberately left vague lest absolute clarity lull the people into complacency.

In describing future events, the prophets often do not follow strict chronological order. Many of the prophets go back and take up ideas which they have already introduced in earlier passages. This means that it is impossible simply to work through a passage in the prophets and assume that the order of events will happen in precisely the same order as they occur in the written prophecy.

When describing events which are far apart in time, the prophets often speak of them as if they were much closer together. Just as we have difficulty in determining any depth dimension when we look at the stars, so we find it difficult to be certain about the length of time separating specific events spoken of in prophecy.

The prophets looked to the Messianic age as such, and did not make any distinction between what we call the first and second comings of Christ. The New Testament clearly distinguishes between the first coming of Jesus and his coming a second time, 'not to bear sin, but to bring salvation to those who are waiting for him' (Heb. 9:28).

Apocalyptic

In addition to prophecy in the Old Testament, there are some parts which are distinctive enough from the rest of prophecy to be called apocalyptic. These passages include the book of Daniel, parts of Ezekiel and Zechariah, and a section of Isaiah which is often called 'the little apocalypse' (Isa. 24-27). Our English word 'apocalyptic' comes from a Greek word which means to reveal, to uncover. It has been used to describe these Old Testament passages and the book of Revelation in the New Testament because it was felt that they were unveiling what was to happen in the future. This understanding of apocalyptic put the stress on teaching about the end time as being the main characteristic of this type of literature. In so doing, there was the suggestion that prophecy and apocalyptic are not really connected with one another. This can be diagrammed in this way:

├──────Prophecy──────┤ ├──────Apocalyptic ──────┤

However, it is truer to say that the apocalyptic literature of the Bible is more concerned with present time rather than with future time. Its aim is to speak to the present and to explain the human situation in terms of what is to happen when God reveals the fullness of his glory and purposes to his saints in heaven. Often there is disclosure of heavenly realities by means of visions which portray the truth of God in a very vivid way. Instead of seeing a sharp distinction between prophecy and apocalyptic, we can diagram the relationship in this way:

├──────Prophecy──────┤
            ├────── Apocalyptic──────┤

Old Testament Apocalypses

In the Old Testament, the book of Daniel stands out as the major example of apocalyptic literature. Daniel was a prophet who ministered in a foreign land. During the closing years of the kingdom of Judah he was among a group of captives carried away to Babylon in 605 BC. Daniel was soon placed in a high administrative position, and successfully served under Nebuchadnezzar, Belshazzar and Darius. The book called by his name consists of two parts. In the first part (chapters 1-6), there is a record of various details in the life of Daniel in Babylon, while the second part (chapters 7-12) contains four visions of Daniel. In these visions, there appears a succession of kingdoms arising on the earth, but also an ultimate kingdom which will last forever.

The period of Daniel was one in which God's people needed comfort and encouragement. Though warned as early as the time of Moses that disobedience would bring banishment from the promised land (see Deut. 28:64; 29:28), the people had not really believed the warnings. Even when the prophets repeated the warnings, they 'mocked God's messengers, despised his words and scoffed at his prophets until the wrath of the LORD was aroused against his people and there was no remedy' (2 Chron. 36:16). The covenant people were expelled from their own land and they were in captivity in Babylon. Many people must have thought that the gods of the army which could raze the temple in Jerusalem to the ground were vastly superior to the God of the Jews. Just as in the days of Moses when God displayed his power over the Egyptians and their gods, so in the time of Daniel he displayed his might by a series of miracles. These miracles set out in Daniel chapters 1-6 show that the living God of Israel was in charge of all human affairs and that he could deliver his people from their bondage.

By means of the visions in the second part of the book, God revealed yet again his sovereign grace and he gave glimpses concerning the future salvation. Daniel was enabled to look forward to the coming of the Messiah, and to encourage the people with the prospect of the ultimate deliverance of God. The book ends with the mention of a mysterious time of waiting 'till the end' (Dan. 12:13). The New Testament apocalypse, the book of Revelation, takes up the message where Daniel leaves off, and points to the final confrontation between God and the forces of evil. The future is secure because 'the kingdom of the world has become the kingdom of our Lord and of his Christ, and he will reign for ever and ever' (Rev. 11:15).

16

THE NEW COVENANT

Covenant History

From the time of the covenant made on Mount Sinai
Israel, as God's people, was expected to live in
obedience to the covenant's demands. With the
introduction of kingship, another facet of the
covenant relationship was stressed in the covenant
with David (2 Sam. 7; Pss. 89; 132). The Davidic
family was chosen to provide the line of kings which
would ultimately culminate in the coming of Jesus.
Throughout the Old Testament period the people
often wandered far from the demands of the
covenant, and one of the major tasks of the prophets
was to call them back to obedience to it. A prophet
like Elijah, in his dejection after reaching Horeb,
could complain to God: 'I have been very zealous
for the LORD God Almighty. The Israelites have
rejected your covenant, broken down your altars,
and put your prophets to death with the sword' (1
Kings 19:10).

Some periods of reformation took place,
particularly those under Hezekiah and Josiah. The
reformation under Josiah is important in itself, but
also because it provides a background for the
teaching of Jeremiah and Ezekiel of a new covenant.
Josiah reigned for 31 years (from 639 to 608 BC),
the first eight of which were probably by means of
a regency until he came of age. The biblical

accounts of his reign are found in 2 Kings 22, 23:1-30 and 2 Chronicles 34 and 35. He adopted an independent policy for Judah which had as its aims

freedom of control from Assyria which had already been responsible for the downfall of the northern kingdom of Israel in 722 BC.

the removal of Assyrian influence in the worship of God (the biblical records concentrate on this aspect of his reign).

the attempt to integrate the northern part of the country, which previously belonged to Israel, into the kingdom of Judah.

Josiah began a work of reformation (2 Chron. 34:3-7), which was given new impetus and direction when 'the book of the law' (probably some or all of the book of Deuteronomy) was found during repairs to the Temple. Even in the midst of this work, a warning was given to king and people that though Josiah himself was going to be spared seeing the final disaster on the nation, yet God's punishment was coming on the people because of their sins (2 Kings 22:15-20). The people of Judah joined in a solemn act of covenant renewal (2 Kings 23:1-3) and they celebrated the Passover in a manner which had not been seen since the days of the judges (2 Kings 23:21-23). But the heart of the people had not really changed at all, and so the prophets started to proclaim a message of a new covenant which God was going to introduce.

The New Covenant

Earlier prophets had spoken of a new relationship with God which God himself would bring about. Prophets such as Hosea and Isaiah depicted a day coming when the worship of idols would cease and God and his people would be bound together for ever. Thus Hosea speaks of a future covenant which God will make, and of the time when he will say 'to those called "Not my people", "You are my people"; and they will say, "You are my God" ' (Hos. 2:23; cf. Paul's use of this passage in Romans 9:25). Isaiah prophesied that the Messiah himself would be the covenant for the people (Isa. 42:6), and that he would confirm the sure promises made to David by means of an everlasting covenant (Isa. 55:3; see also Isa. 61:8; Jer. 32:40, 50:5; Ezek. 16:60; 37:26). The idea of 'newness' is brought out by Ezekiel's references to a 'new heart' or a 'new spirit' to be given to the people by God (Ezek. 11:19; 18:31; 36:26), just as the psalms which speak of the coming judge call for a 'new song' (Pss. 96, 98).

It is, however, in Jeremiah 31:31-34 that we have the fullest statement of the New Covenant. Jeremiah was a prophet during the reign of King Josiah. He was called to the office of prophet in the thirteenth year of King Josiah (626 BC), and prophesied until the fall of Jerusalem in 586 BC. The great theme of his prophecy was the judgment of God directed against Judah, especially in the form of the invading Babylonian army. He tried to call the people back to obedience to the then existing covenant, saying:

'Listen to the terms of this covenant and follow them' (Jer. 11:6). He realised that the reforms under Josiah, while good in themselves, had not changed the basic condition of the people. In a prophecy specifically dated as being in the days of King Josiah, Jeremiah speaks the Lord's condemnation of Judah because the lessons manifest in the fall of the northern kingdom of Israel had not been taken to heart (Jer. 3:6-10). The situation required something more than just re-affirmation of the existing covenant. What was needed was a covenant which was new in character as well as new in time. Jeremiah gives a picture of days coming when God will institute a new covenant. The Lord declared: 'I will put my law in their minds and write it on their hearts. I will be their God, and they will be my people' (Jer. 31:33). This assurance of God's special relationship with them, expressed in the oft-repeated covenant formula of the Old Testament, pointed to continuity with the past, just as there were other elements which directed attention to what was new. Several things were intended by this new covenant.

The new covenant would mean that God would implant his law in the hearts of his people. What was needed was not just better memories, but a new nature! Only God could give a heart liberated from bondage to sin and able spontaneously to respond to his commands.

The new covenant would be a matter of personal experience of the living God. The relationship with God was not just to be on national terms, but it was to be a very personal matter. Every member of the covenant community would possess knowledge of the Lord because of their new heart.

The new covenant was to involve God granting his forgiveness and not remembering their sins any more. Clearly, forgiveness was taught elsewhere and earlier in the Old Testament. But this prophecy looks forward to the day when God would act through the death of the Messiah to do something to blot out his people's sins for ever. Under the Old Testament sacrifices there was remembrance of sins every year (Heb. 10:3). Under the new covenant there is no such remembrance because of a sacrifice which was made once for all (Heb. 7:27).

The prophecy of Jeremiah 31 came to fulfilment in the ministry and death of Jesus. It is the passage which suggested to Origen in the early church that the last twenty-seven books of the Bible should be called 'the New Testament'. This prophecy is the largest passage of the Old Testament to be quoted in the New Testament (Heb. 8:8-12, and partially repeated in Heb. 10:16-17). It also occurs in passages dealing with the Lord's Supper (Matt.

26:28; Mark 14:24; Luke 22:20; 1 Cor. 11:25). Jesus' death inaugurated the new covenant, one which transcends the old boundaries of Israel and Judah and embraces believers of all nations.

17

EXILE AND RETURN

Exile from the Promised Land

The threat of exile was given to the children of Israel by Moses, even before they entered into the land. In addition to the threat of invading armies besieging them, Moses explained that if the Lord's commands were not heeded, the people would be scattered among the nations (Lev. 26:27-33, Deut. 28:64ff.). That warning was taken up and set before the people by several of the Old Testament prophets (e.g. Amos, Micah, Hosea, Isaiah). Thus Isaiah spoke of the desolation of the land which was coming, when God would send everyone far away (Isa. 6:11ff.). He also described the results of the impending Assyrian invasion (Isa. 7:18ff.; 8:1-10).

The Fall of Israel (the Northern Kingdom)

The northern kingdom of Israel was the first of the two parts of the nation to fall. The Assyrians gradually encroached on Israelite territory as Israel's power declined. Hoshea, the last king, revolted against Assyria and refused to pay the annual tribute money (2 Kings 17:3-4). The Assyrians marched on Israel in 724 BC, and though the Assyrians expected the city of Samaria to yield quickly to a siege, it managed to hold out until it finally fell in 722 BC. An Assyrian governor was placed over the land, many Israelites were deported, and foreign settlers were brought in (2 Kings 17:24). Israel had existed as a separate nation for over two centuries (from 931 to 722 BC), but now ceased for ever to be a sovereign power.

The Fall of Judah (the Southern Kingdom)
The southern kingdom of Judah was to last for another 130 years. Just prior to its downfall, the Babylonians under Nebuchadnezzar in 605 BC had become the major power. Jerusalem was captured in 596 BC, and about 10,000 people from Judah were taken away captive (2 Kings 24:14-16). Zedekiah was installed and ruled for a time, before he revolted against his overlord. Jeremiah had constantly spoken of the final doom which was coming, and in accord with his word Jerusalem fell finally in 587. In addition to the very full accounts in the biblical text (2 Kings 25; 2 Chron. 36:15-21; Jer. 52), letters from the military outpost at Lachish (south-west of Jerusalem) give graphic details of the Babylonian invasion. Jerusalem was devastated, and all but the poor of the land were seized and deported (2 Kings 25:11-12, 22). That the number of deportees had to be quite large is shown by the numbers who returned from captivity in 538.

The kingdoms of Israel and Judah did not fall simply because they were too weak to withstand the major powers like Assyria and Babylon. The biblical writers declare that it was because of the sins of the people that God permitted this to happen.

Israel had practised idolatry, worshipped the stars, and sacrificed sons and daughters in the fire (2 Kings 17:7-17), all of which were a rejection of God's covenant demands (v. 15). The invasion of Judah by the Babylonians is said to have been God's purpose to destroy Judah 'in accordance with the word of the LORD proclaimed by his servants the prophets' (2 Kings 24:2). The land then had the opportunity to enjoy its Sabbath rest for seventy years in order to fulfil Moses' warning (Lev. 26:34, 43; repeated by Jeremiah, Jer. 29:10). It could then have what the people had failed in their sin to give it during their years of occupation. The reason why the smaller and weaker southern kingdom of Judah lasted longer than Israel cannot be explained in human terms. It was solely because the family of David was the divinely appointed royal household of Judah and because of God's choice of Jerusalem that Judah lasted longer.

Conditions in Exile

The cream of the Jewish population was deported to Babylon, but yet the captivity experienced was not oppressive in many respects. The Jews had freedom of movement, and they were able to engage in trade, commerce and crafts. Perhaps the influence of Daniel at the Babylonian court may account for the generally favourable conditions under which the Israelites lived. They lived by the river (or canal) Kebar (Ezek. 1:1), which was the source of irrigation for the rich farming area. Contact was maintained with Palestine by correspondence (cf. Jer. 29), and messengers were also able to bring information such as the fall of Jerusalem (see Ezek. 33:21-22). As the opening of Jeremiah's letter shows, their own office-bearers such as prophets, elders and priests were still active even in captivity.

The reality of the exile experience was, however, pressed home to the people, and they knew that it was a punishment by God. Certainly in the early years they felt deeply the experience of being severed from Jerusalem and all its religious associations. Psalm 137 records how they wept when, by the rivers of Babylon, they thought about Zion. The book of Lamentations also records the outpourings of a devout heart in the face of the destruction of Jerusalem. The poet speaks of how God has deserted his sanctuary and allowed evil forces to destroy it. The sin of the people had brought this destruction to pass. The small prophecy of Obadiah most probably comes from this period. Obadiah refers to the sin of the Edomites in rejoicing at their brother's fall, which point is referred to in Psalm 137:7 ('Remember, O LORD, what the Edomites did on the day Jerusalem fell. "Tear it down," they cried, "tear it down to its foundations!"'). Even after Jerusalem had fallen, the exiles found it difficult to understand the need for spiritual change and obedience to the Lord (Ezek. 33:30-33).

The Return from Captivity

Repeatedly the prophets had spoken of the fact that God was going to bring Israel and Judah back from their captivity. Isaiah in particular had described not only a return to Palestine but also a return to the mighty God (Isa. 10:21). In his later pictures of the return he describes the new exodus which is going to take place, when God brings his people through the desert to the promised land. Both Jeremiah and Ezekiel prophesied concerning the return, with Ezekiel stressing the return of one nation, under one king (Ezek. 37:1-28). Not only were there general prophecies depicting the return, but Isaiah went further and spoke of the specific manner in which God would accomplish this. He said that God would raise up an anointed servant called Cyrus who would permit the return and the rebuilding of the Temple (Isa. 44:28-45:7).

Cyrus the Persian captured Babylon in 539 BC and in 538 he issued a decree permitting the return of the Jews (see 2 Chron. 36:22-23; Ezra 1:1-4). This marked the end of the period of exile. The actual return took place in three phases, and these were characterised by

the return in 537 under Sheshbazzar, and, after opposition, the completion of the rebuilding of the Temple (Ezra 1-6). The prophets of this stage were Haggai and Zechariah, who encouraged the people in their work on the Temple.

the return in 458 under Ezra and his reforms, especially in the area of mixed marriages (Ezra 7-10). The book of Esther is dated in the period just prior to this return and gives a picture of Jewish life under Persian rule.

the final return under Nehemiah in 444, and the rebuilding of the walls of Jerusalem (Ezra 4:6-23; Neh. 1–12). The last prophet of the Old Testament, Malachi, most probably worked in the period of Nehemiah.

The joy of the returning exiles is captured in Psalm 126. For them it was like a dream to have been restored by the Lord to their own land. They could sing: 'The LORD has done great things for us, and we are filled with joy' (v. 3).

18

THE PROMISED MESSIAH

Expecting the Messiah

Some believers in the period just before Jesus' birth had a strong sense of expectancy regarding the coming of the Messiah. The aged Simeon had been told that he would not die before he saw the Lord's Christ (Luke 2:26). Similarly, Anna spoke of the birth of Jesus to all who were looking for God's redemption (Luke 2:38). But the expectation was far wider than just with a small group of devout worshippers. Many Jewish people were looking for the appearance of the Messiah (in Greek, the Christ), though they disputed whether Jesus was indeed that person. John 7:25ff. records incidents concerning Jesus' public ministry. Some of the people responded to his teaching by claiming he was the Christ. Others said: 'How can the Christ come from Galilee? Does not the Scripture say that the Christ will come from David's family and from Bethlehem, the town where David lived?' (vv. 41-42).

During his ministry Jesus taught that people should have known about his coming because they had the writings of the Old Testament. Because he clearly made himself equal with God by his teaching, the Jews were roused to anger. In replying to them Jesus said: 'You diligently study the Scriptures because you think that by them you possess eternal life. These are the Scriptures that testify about me, yet you refuse to come to me to have life' (John 5:39-40). Jesus repeatedly spoke of the fact that the Old Testament Scriptures expressly taught about his coming and his mission. After his resurrection, in speaking with Cleopas and his friend on the road to Emmaus, Jesus began with Moses and all the prophets and explained what was said in all the Scriptures about himself (Luke 24:27). A little later to the assembled disciples he said: 'Everything must be fulfilled that is written about me in the Law of Moses, the Prophets and the Psalms' (Luke 24:44).

Pointers to the Messiah
Throughout the Old Testament there were various signposts directing people to the coming of a deliverer. From the earliest promise in Genesis 3:15 onwards, God indicated in various ways that he was going to save his people. As the centuries passed it was more clearly revealed that this was to be done through an individual figure, anointed for the particular mission on which he would be sent. The Hebrew word for 'anointed' has been taken over into English as 'Messiah', while our word 'Christ' is simply the Greek equivalent. In Jacob's blessing of his sons, he indicated that the sceptre was not going to depart from the tribe of Judah until the one came to whom tribute belonged (Gen. 49:10), Similarly, in another cryptic statement Balaam spoke of his vision of a star coming out of Jacob (Num. 24:17).

Alongside such earlier prophecies we have to consider the role played by the sacrificial system in Israel. In the sacrifices Israel had picture language, which taught them about the reality of sins forgiven, but which also pointed them ahead to a far greater sacrifice for sins. The constant repetition of sacrifices demonstrated their inability to take away sins. What was needed was for God in his grace to provide a single sacrifice for sin which would not need any repetition. The prophets spoke of a glorious day in the future when God himself would open up a fountain to cleanse the people from their impurity and sin (Zech. 13:1). This was fulfilled when Jesus died once for all for the sins of his people (Heb. 7:27).

The offices of prophet, priest and king also pointed forward to someone who would both realise each office to its fullest extent and also combine them in one person. The holders of these offices in the Old Testament period were all imperfect, but yet the offices pointed away from the occupants to the coming fulfilment. The New Testament tells how they were all fulfilled in Jesus. He came as the last of a long line of prophetic messengers (Matt. 21:33-45) and so was the culmination of the promise of a prophet like Moses (Deut. 18:18; Acts 3:22-23). As a priest, Jesus was not only the offerer of a sacrifice, but he himself was that sacrifice. Peter points to this fact when he says that Christ 'himself bore our sin in his body on the tree, so that we might die to sins and live for righteousness' (1 Pet. 2:24).

To Jesus as king all authority has been given (Matt. 28:18), and he must reign until all his enemies are subdued under his feet (1 Cor. 15:25).

The Suffering Servant

All the early indications in the Old Testament of a coming saviour were made explicit by the great prophets of the 8th century BC. Amos and Hosea, Micah and Isaiah unite in their predictions concerning an individual Messianic figure. On many occasions they use language from earlier in the Old Testament and show how it relates to the promised Messiah. Hosea spoke of a period when the Israelites would lack a king, and then they would 'return and seek the LORD their God and David their king' (Hos. 3:4-5). Amos also connects the family of David with the coming days of blessing (Amos 9:11-12), while Micah told of a ruler over Israel who was going to come from Bethlehem Judah (Mic. 5:2). King Herod heard of this passage when he enquired of the priests and teachers where the Christ should be born. 'In Bethlehem in Judea', they answered, and then quoted this verse from Micah (Matt. 2:1-6). But above all the other prophets Isaiah proclaimed most fully the character and work of the coming Messiah. At a crucial point in Judah's history he prophesied of a virgin who would bear a son to be called Immanuel, God-with-us (Isa. 7:14). That child was going to bear names which belong only to God, for he was to be Wonderful Counsellor, Mighty God, Everlasting Father, Prince of Peace.

Moreover, his task was described in kingly terms and he was to sit on David's throne (Isa. 9:6-7). This coming ruler from the stump of Jesse would rule righteously and gather many nations under his banner (Isa. 11:1ff.).

Isaiah describes very fully in the Servant Songs the role of this special servant whom God would anoint as his Messiah. These songs are found in Isaiah 42:1-9, 49:1-13, 50:4-11, and 52:13-53:12. The term 'servant of the Lord' is used in the Old Testament very rarely. It is applied to special servants such as Moses and David, and sometimes even to the nation as a whole. But as Isaiah's prophecies proceed we hear him speaking of an individual who is truly Israel and who pours out his soul to death for many (Isa. 53:12). The last great servant song gives us five pictures of the promised Messiah.

It summarises the priestly work which the Messiah will carry out (Isa. 52:13-15).

It speaks of unbelief when he appears and of his unpromising appearance (Isa. 53:1-3).

It describes him as a substitute for sinners who have wandered away (Isa. 53:4-6).

It tells of his submissiveness and purity, even in death (Isa. 53:7-9).

It predicts his successful intercession (Isa. 53:10-12).

The focal point of both Old and New Testament is the same – Jesus, the Saviour. In answer to a question from the Ethiopian official about Isaiah 53, 'Philip began with that very passage of Scripture and told him the good news about Jesus' (Acts 8:35). As Augustine put it: 'The New is in the Old concealed; the Old is in the New revealed.' Study of the Old Testament must always lead us to Christ and to that gospel which God 'promised beforehand through his prophets in the Holy Scriptures regarding his Son, who as to his human nature was a descendant of David' (Rom. 1:2-3).